The Musician's Guide to
Audio

MUSICIAN'S GUIDE TO
homerec rding

The Musician's Guide to Audio

Audio

Craig Anderton

Hal Leonard Books
An Imprint of Hal Leonard LLC

Published in 2019 by Hal Leonard Books
An Imprint of Hal Leonard LLC
7777 West Bluemound Road
Milwaukee, WI 53213

Trade Book Division Editorial Offices
33 Plymouth St., Montclair, NJ 07042

The following photo is provided courtesy of University of Rochester: Urnano: Figure 1.3.

The following photo is provided courtesy of Sweetwater.com: Figures 2.15.

Printed in the United States of America

Book design by NextPoint Training, Inc.

Library of Congress Cataloging-in-Publication Data is available upon request.

ISBN 978-1-5400-2692-7

www.halleonardbooks.com

Contents

Acknowledgments

A series like this is never the work of one person, but rather a collection of the experiences obtained over the years from too many people to acknowledge here. Yet some deserve a special mention.

Dan Earley, my editor at Music Sales, who was the first person to say, "You know what would be cool? A series of books on recording, like those Time Life libraries." Well Dan, better late than never, right?

Sir George Martin, who was kind enough to write the foreword to my 1977 book, *Home Recording for Musicians*. He asked for samples of my writing, and I thought that would be the end of it. Instead, he wrote an eloquent foreword that set a wonderful tone for the book. He truly was the consummate gentleman everyone says he was.

The team at Hal Leonard—especially John Cerullo, who green-lighted this series and brought in Frank D. Cook to serve as the editor for these books.

My father, who taught me that it didn't matter if I was a dreadful writer as long as I could edit my words into something readable—and who also showed me what it meant to love music.

My mother, who with my father was unfailingly supportive when I wanted to do things like drop out of college, join a rock band, go on tour, and never look back!

My brother, who understood music on a very deep level and died too young.

And of course, the many *(many)* engineers and producers who let me look over their shoulders and absorb knowledge like a sponge over the past five decades. My hope is that this series will help pass their collective wisdom on to another generation.

About This Book

Welcome to the book series Musician's Guide to Home Recording. This series of short publications was written to address the needs of musicians and recording enthusiasts who are interested in creating self-produced songs or doing audio production work for others.

Rather than trying to cover all aspects of recording in a single sprawling volume, each title in the series concisely and accessibly addresses a particular subject. You can select individual titles to hone in on certain skills or proceed through the entire series; this kind of approach lets you develop a comprehensive knowledge at your own pace.

This book, *The Musician's Guide to Audio,* is essential reading to understand the analog and digital technology behind today's audio tools.

Getting the Most out of Your Audio

Digital audio's impact on home recording cannot be overstated—recording used to mean paying for expensive studio time or spending tens of thousands of dollars (or more!) to create your own studio. But no more. Thanks to digital technology, it's possible to have a laptop computer-based studio whose capabilities far exceed "big" studios of only a few decades ago.

However, digital audio is still a relatively young technology. While analog recording is a mature field, the technology and products associated with digital audio continue to progress. And though it would be great if digital audio were simply "plug and play," it's not always that simple. There are many nuances to digital audio, and the ways to get the most out of your audio aren't always obvious.

Along with analog audio, this book focuses on digital audio as it relates to home recording: strengths, limitations, techniques, ways to improve audio quality, and much more. If you want to go deep into the technical rabbit hole, you'll find endless debates online about extremely arcane aspects of digital audio. We're not going to go there; instead, we'll cover what you need to know to make music. However, I have included various "Tech Talk" sidebars that can get pretty deep into the weeds if you want more detail on particular topics.

In any event, the more you know about the technology behind the scenes, the more easily you can take advantage of it to do your bidding—and to make better music.

Tips and References

This book includes various tips, definitions, cross-references, and other supplemental nuggets throughout its pages. These are denoted with the following icons and formatting.

 Tips and side notes provide helpful hints and suggestions, background information, or additional details on a concept or topic.

 Definitions provide explanations of technical terms, industry jargon, or abbreviations.

 Cross-References alert you to another section, book, or online resource that provides additional information on the current topic.

<h1 style="text-align:center">Chapter 1</h1>

Introduction to Audio

The art of sound recording and reproduction, whose fundamentals had remained essentially unchanged for decades, underwent a radical transformation in the 1980s due to the introduction of low-cost digital technology. This technology—which brought us home computers, digital wristwatches, smart phones, car navigation systems that talk to you, and other modern miracles—has re-shaped the way we record, mix, edit, and listen to music.

The promise of digital audio is the potential for quality sound, whether the medium is streaming audio, a digital sampling keyboard, a delay line, a computer-based recording system, or a consumer item such as a compact disc. Also, because much research and development is dedicated to lowering the cost of computer technology while improving performance, and digital audio uses much of the same technology, digital audio equipment continues to become less expensive, while quality continues to improve.

Analog Audio Basics

Sound consists of variations in air pressure, which interact with our ears' hearing mechanism. The information received by our ears travels to the brain, where this information is processed. The most common analogy to sound is ocean waves, which are created primarily by wind variations. Like ocean waves, sound waves have *crests* (the highest point in the wave's cycle) and *troughs* (the lowest point in the wave's cycle). The wave's height is its *amplitude*—for example, the crest has a higher amplitude than the trough. The rate at which these waves occur is their *frequency*.

Acoustic instruments, by their very nature, generate changes in air pressure that we hear directly as sound. Electronic instruments create their sound in the form of voltage variations. These voltage variations must be converted into moving air so we can hear them. This requires a *transducer*, the name for a device that converts one form of energy into another. For example, a loudspeaker converts voltage variations into air pressure variations (the speaker cone moving back and forth creates these variations). A microphone changes air pressure that hits a thin diaphragm into voltage variations. Other transducers include guitar pickups (which convert the mechanical energy of vibrating strings to electrical energy), and phono cartridges (which convert side-to-side stylus motion into electrical energy).

All audio, from a barking dog to a symphony orchestra, is a wave with a varying level. Often, the more complex the sound, the more complex the shape of the wave. Visually, when presented on a graph of amplitude (level) versus time, audio looks like a squiggly line that's called a *waveform* (Fig. 1.1).

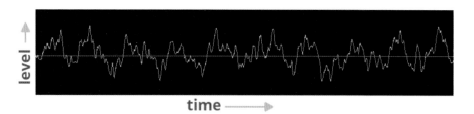

Figure 1.1 This graph shows air pressure changes created by an orchestra (playing a Beethoven symphony), after being converted into a varying voltage by a microphone. Note that this is a very short piece of audio—zooming in shows the waveform's shape more clearly.

The waveform could represent air pressure changes, voltage changes, string motion across a pickup, etc. A straight horizontal line represents a condition of no change (e.g., zero air pressure or voltage, as shown by the orange line in Fig. 1.1), and the waveform's level references this base line. For example, if the waveform is showing a speaker cone's motion, excursions above the base line indicate that the speaker cone is moving outward, while excursions below the base line indicate that the speaker cone is moving inward. These excursions could just as easily represent a fluctuating voltage (such as a signal coming out of a synthesizer) that alternates between positive and negative, or the air pressure changes that occur when you strike a piano key.

In some multitrack recording programs, a waveform's visual representation fills in the space between the line that represents audio and the line that represents a condition of no change (Fig. 1.2). This makes it easier to see waveform shapes with lots of tracks, because the height for each waveform decreases as you add more tracks. However, the waveform is still a single, varying level.

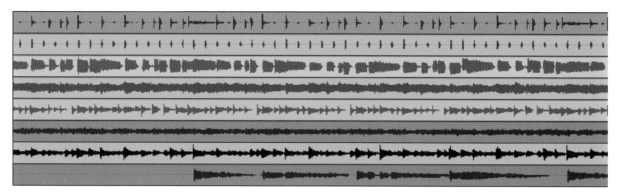

Figure 1.2 Waveforms are often "filled in" visually with multitrack recording software. Note that these are all monaural (not stereo) tracks.

Analog Audio Recording and Playback: Vinyl and Tape

If we carve a waveform's outline into a vinyl record, the record's groove will trace that waveform's shape (Fig. 1.3).

Figure 1.3 This image of vinyl record grooves was done by Chris Supranowitz, using a scanning electron microscope.

When we play a record, the stylus traces this waveform, and the phono cartridge generates voltage variations that are analogous to the sound's original air pressure changes. This low-level signal then passes through a preamplifier, and finally a power amplifier, which increases the voltage level enough to drive a speaker. Because the speaker cone follows the waveform motion, it reproduces the same air variations originally pressed into the vinyl record. Notice that each stage transfers a signal in its own medium (vinyl, wire, air, etc.) that's analogous to the input signal—hence the term, *analog* audio.

With tape recording, the process isn't as obvious as when carving a waveform into plastic. Instead, a tape recorder's *record head* is a transducer that converts audio into magnetic energy. The record head impresses magnetic patterns on tape that represents the audio waveform. On playback, a playback head converts the magnetic energy back into a voltage, which then works its way eventually to speakers or headphones.

Analog Audio Drawbacks

Unfortunately, analog audio has multiple flaws, which helped drive the movement toward digital audio. For example, if a vinyl record has pops, clicks, warps, or surface noise, these will be added to the original sound, and you'll hear them as undesirable audio "artifacts" in the output. A phono cartridge will also add its own coloration; and if it can't follow rapid changes due to mechanical inertia, distortion will result.

Amplifiers add noise and hum, speakers are subject to various types of distortion, tape recording has hiss and *non-linearities* (e.g., the output waveform may not look like the input waveform), and so on. So, while the signal appearing at a speaker's output may be very similar to what was originally recorded, it will not duplicate the original sound exactly, due to the types of errors inherent in analog recording, processing, and playback. When you copy a master tape or press it into vinyl, other problems will occur due to the flawed nature of the transfer process. When you copy an analog recording, the copy's sound quality will not be as good as the source.

Digital Audio Basics

Digital audio removes some of the variables from the recording and playback process by converting audio into a string of numbers and then passing these numbers through the audio chain (we'll soon explain why this improves the sound). Figure 1.4 illustrates the conversion process from an analog signal into a digital number, which is the job of an *analog-to-digital converter* (ADC or A/D converter for short). Figure 1.4A shows a waveform that will end up being converted to digital data.

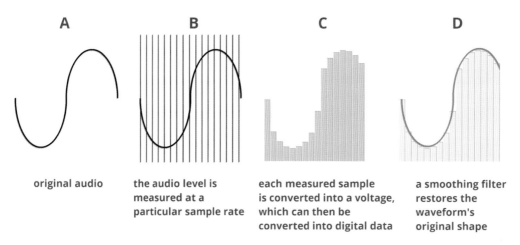

A	B	C	D
original audio	the audio level is measured at a particular sample rate	each measured sample is converted into a voltage, which can then be converted into digital data	a smoothing filter restores the waveform's original shape

Figure 1.4 The process of analog-to-digital conversion samples a waveform at a consistent rate and measures the level of each sample.

A computer takes a "snapshot" of the signal every few microseconds (1/1,000,000th of a second—see Fig. 1.4B). This series of snapshots, or *samples*, represent voltage levels that trace the signal's level variations (Fig. 1.4C). The computer then converts the measured levels into a string of numbers (in the form of digital data) that specify the voltage variations. The number of measurements the converter takes each second is the *sample rate*, also called *sampling frequency*.

Let's relate what we've discussed so far to a typical audio system. A traditional microphone picks up an audio signal and sends it to the ADC for conversion to digital. The computer takes this string of digital information and processes it—for example, delays it before playing it back to create a digital delay, or stores it on a hard disk for digital recording.

So far so good, but listening to a bunch of numbers isn't a wonderful audio experience. We need to convert this string of numbers back into an analog signal that can drive a loudspeaker or headphones. A *digital-to-analog converter* (DAC or D/A converter) provides this function by converting the numerical samples back to a series of voltage levels.

However, we're not done yet, because we need to smooth that series of discrete voltages into a continuous waveform. A *low-pass* filter works in conjunction with the DAC to filter the stair-step signal, rounding off the sharp edges (Fig. 1.4D). We can then take this newly converted analog signal and send it through an amplifier/speaker combination.

Although this might seem complex, it provides several advantages compared to analog audio, as covered next.

How Digital Audio Maintains Fidelity

A digitally encoded signal is not subject to the same kind of deterioration as analog audio. Consider the compact disc; it stores digital data on a plastic disc. A laser reads this data and then sends it to a DAC to convert it back into analog. By taking this approach, if a minor scratch appears on the disc, it doesn't really matter—the system recognizes only numbers, so it won't recognize the scratch as a number. When downloading music, even if there's a momentary interruption in your internet connection, a properly designed download engine will assemble the pieces into a file that you can play back without interruption.

Even more importantly for musicians, using digital audio preserves quality as the audio goes through the signal chain. For example, in the days of analog multitrack recorders, a song was mixed down to an analog two-track tape, which introduced some sound degradation due to limits of the two-track machine. It then was mastered (another chance for error), was converted into a metal stamper (where even more errors could occur), and finally was pressed into a record (where problems could occur like pops, record wear, and warping). At each audio transfer stage, the signal quality deteriorated.

With digital recording, when it's time to mix down, you mix down the numbers to stereo or surround, which creates another set of numbers. (Of course, these numbers also go through a DAC for monitoring purposes so you can hear the sound through speakers or headphones.) As a result, the stereo mix will represent exactly what you heard when you mixed the song. Next, you can take that digitally mixed string of numbers and stream it from the net, copy it over to a smartphone's memory, press the bits into a compact disc, and so on. In each case, unless you choose to use *data compression* to reduce the file size, any transfer is a clone of the original sound that doesn't deteriorate along the way.

 Chapter 5 of this book covers the subject of data compression in detail.

You can think of the ADC at the signal chain's beginning as "freeze drying" the sound, which is not reconstituted until it hits the DAC in a playback system. This is why digital audio can sound so clean: it hasn't been subjected to the petty humiliations an analog signal endures as it works its way from studio to home stereo speaker.

Digital Audio Issues

Although analog technology isn't perfect, neither is digital—but the issues are different. We'll explore potential problems and solutions in depth throughout this book, but here's a quick overview:

♦ **Sampling rate issues.** If the system doesn't take samples of the signal level at a fast enough rate, it's harder to reproduce the signal accurately. The sampling rate has to be at least twice the frequency of the highest audio frequency entering the system.

♦ **Output filter coloration.** As mentioned, a post-DAC low-pass filter converts the stair-step samples into a smooth, continuous signal. However, a filter may add its own coloration.

♦ **Resolution (quantization) errors.** Another sampling issue relates to *resolution* accuracy. If a digital audio system can measure levels within an accuracy of 10 millivolts (mV, or 1/100th of a volt), a level of 10 mV would be assigned one number, a level of 20 mV another number, a level of 30 mV yet another number, and so on. Now suppose the computer tries to measure a 15 mV signal—the computer can't resolve that value, so it has to assign a value of either 10 mV or 20 mV. In either case, the sample does not correspond exactly to the original input level, which produces an error. Actual accuracies are *far* better than this example, but it's still possible for errors to creep in.

♦ **We live in the real world.** Manufacturing processes aren't perfect; sometimes corners are cut to reach a price point, and factors like circuit board layout—and even the power supply that powers a device—can influence sound quality.

Regardless of its limitations, many musicians feel that the *potential* for subtle errors in digital recording is preferable to the restrictions of analog recording. So while digital audio may not be perfect, it's pretty close. Besides, even several decades after its introduction, digital audio technology continues to improve.

Tech Talk: The Clone Controversy

Some people insist that digital copies, despite being theoretically identical to their source, can sound different—in other words, if you take a CD and clone it, it might not sound the same as the original. But digital just doesn't work that way; copying a series of numbers produces the same series of numbers. Granted, CDs have error correction algorithms to compensate for issues that could crop up during manufacturing or playback, but even error correction won't change the sound unless the errors are *so* significant that the error correction algorithm has to create a new signal to replace audio it can't reconstruct. You can clone digital data all day—compare the numeric stream of numbers, and they'll be identical.

One possible reason why people hear a difference could be the test procedure. For example, playing back two clones on two different systems may subject them to subtle differences in the two systems' electronics. Another, more esoteric possibility is that the sound being monitored during the recording process is different compared to playback. This is not necessarily an illusion; *jitter* (caused by running the signal through long cables, as well as by slight sync mismatches between units) results in the numbers arriving at a digital input at slightly varying times, although they are still sent in the correct order so this doesn't affect the clone's quality. On playback, these numbers are lined up with crystal-controlled precision by the device's playback electronics, thus minimizing any jitter.

Jitter is a subtle effect, but it may be significant enough for those with really good ears to notice a difference in the sound between recording and playback. Regardless, that's just a temporary condition, and a clone is a clone.

Frequency, Period, and Wavelength

Audio with repetitive amplitude changes will have a particular *frequency.* The duration of the repeating waveform, called the *period,* determines the frequency (Fig. 1.5). Shorter periods represent higher frequencies.

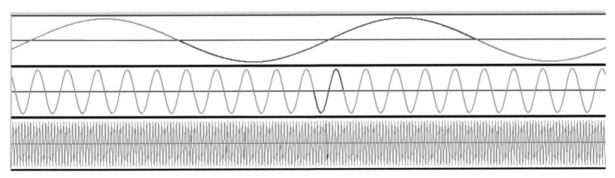

Figure 1.5 The upper waveform is 100 Hz, the middle waveform is 1,000 Hz, and the lower waveform is 10,000 Hz. Each waveform's period is highlighted in red.

Each period is called a *cycle.* Frequency was once denoted in cycles per second (CPS), but was changed in the 60s to hertz (abbreviated Hz) to commemorate Heinrich Rudolf Hertz (1857–1894), the scientist who provided proof that electromagnetic waves exist. Kilohertz (abbreviated kHz) represent one thousand cycles per second. The range of human hearing for a young, healthy adult is approximately 20 Hz to 20 kHz; however, high-frequency response diminishes with age, and abuse from loud sounds can damage hearing at specific frequencies.

In addition to frequency and period, a wave's *wavelength*—the distance a single cycle travels as it moves through the air, or if you prefer, the distance over which that single cycle repeats—also matters for home recording. This is because when you're listening to music in a room, the sound waves bounce off the walls and reflect back into the room. The reflections can interfere with each other in various ways. If the reflection is *in phase* with the waveform (in other words, the crests and troughs line up), the waveforms add together and increase the level. If the reflection is *out of phase* (the crest in one waveform lines up with the trough in the other waveform), the waveforms will cancel to some degree (Fig. 1.6). Ideally, you want acoustic treatment to minimize reflections so you hear only the direct waveform.

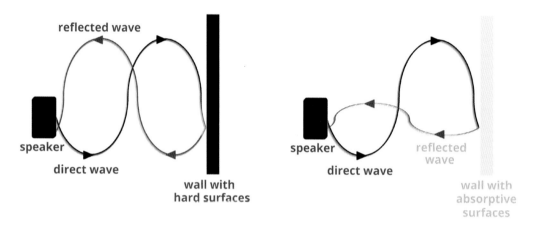

Figure 1.6 In the left view, the direct wave is reflecting off a hard surface, so the reflected wave still has a lot of level. Although the reflected wave isn't completely out of phase with the direct wave, it's mostly equal and opposite, so there will be some cancellation. In the right view, the wall has been treated to absorb sound. The reflected wave is much weaker, so it won't cancel the direct signal as much.

In a small room, there isn't enough space for a low-frequency waveform to develop, because it will bounce off a wall before the cycle has time to complete. As a result, low frequencies often cancel and exhibit other response anomalies. This is why mixes done in small rooms can be bass-heavy, because the person doing the mix will boost the bass to compensate for the bad acoustics. But when that mix is played back in a room with better acoustics, the bass will seem excessively loud.

Acoustical treatment that "traps" reflections or diffuses the sound can help create a more accurate listening environment and a more uniform bass response. Note that listening to a mix through headphones removes the influence of room acoustics, but it alters the sound in other ways (e.g., it can exaggerate the stereo spread compared to speakers).

Tech Talk: Calculating a Frequency's Period and Wavelength

The formula to convert from frequency to period is:

1 / Frequency in Hz = Period in seconds

Each cycle has an associated wavelength that specifies how much distance that cycle covers as it moves through the air (at approximately 331.2 meters or 1,087 feet per second—air pressure, humidity, and temperature can cause slight variations). The formula to calculate wavelength is:

Wavelength = Speed in meters per second / Frequency in Hz

For example, a 50 Hz wave's period covers 331.2/50 = 6.624 meters (about 22 feet) in one second. A 5 kHz wave's period covers 0.066 meters or 6.6 centimeters (about 2.6 inches) in one second.

About Waveforms and Harmonics

As mentioned earlier, sound is like an ocean wave, except that it moves through air instead of water. Unlike a typical ocean wave, though, a sound wave can take on a variety of very different shapes, as represented by its waveform.

The simplest waveform is called a *sine wave*. All its energy is at a *fundamental frequency*. Some waveforms also generate *harmonics*—additional, higher-frequency sounds that relate mathematically to the fundamental frequency. You can classify harmonics as *even* or *odd* harmonics (their mathematical relationship to the fundamental is an even or odd number, respectively). For example, if a fundamental frequency of 1,000 Hz has a harmonic at 2,000 Hz, then this second harmonic would be an even harmonic. A third harmonic at 3,000 Hz would be an odd harmonic.

The number of harmonics, and their levels, affect the waveform's shape and sound. A single cycle of a sine wave, with no harmonics, has a waveform that looks like two half-ovals (Fig. 1.7). If a waveform has only odd harmonics, this produces a "hollow" sound. One cycle of this waveform looks like two squares, hence the name *square* wave. A *triangle* wave also consists of only odd harmonics, but has fewer high-frequency ones. A waveform with a combination of even and odd harmonics is a *sawtooth* wave.

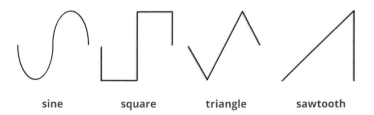

sine   square   triangle   sawtooth

Figure 1.7 Single cycles of sine, square, triangle, and sawtooth waveforms

All harmonics are sine waves that are "mixed" in with the fundamental frequency. In fact (and it took me a while to wrap my head around this), *all* sound can be broken down to a number of sine waves of varying frequencies and amplitudes that end up as a single waveform whose level changes may nonetheless be very complex. This collection of sine waves is called a *Fourier series*, in honor of the French scientist Jean-Baptiste Joseph Fourier (1768–1830). There's even a type of synthesis called *additive synthesis* that creates sounds by adding together sine waves with different frequencies and amplitudes, modified by different attack and decay times.

It may seem this is all of academic interest only, but it's not. For example, the type of harmonics a synthesizer generates can interfere with the process of sampling digital audio, as described later in Chapter 4. Waveforms like square waves (or digital data steams, for that matter) with super-fast rise times need systems with a fast response to reproduce those rise times. You'll see mentions of harmonics and fundamental frequencies as we venture further into the world of audio.

Key Takeaways

- Sound consists of variations in air pressure. Analog audio represents these variations as voltages, while digital audio represents them as numbers.

- Analog audio is subject to degradation at every step of the recording and playback process, whereas digital audio's main issues happen only when an analog signal is being converted to digital, or a digital signal is being converted back to analog again.

- An analog-to-digital converter measures an incoming audio signal at a high rate (tens or even hundreds of thousands of times per second), and translates these measurements into a string of numbers (digital data).

- A digital-to-analog converter translates that string of numbers back into audio that we can hear, after suitable amplification.

- Audio with a repetitive waveform has a particular frequency. The duration of each repetitive waveform is called the period, which is measured in hertz (Hz), also known as cycles-per-second. The distance a cycle travels through air is the wavelength.

- Identical waveforms can be in phase, in which case their levels add, or out of phase, where their levels are equal and opposite and therefore, cancel. Waveforms that aren't identical can be partially in or out of phase, and have partial addition or cancellation.

- Waveforms typically have a fundamental frequency, but can also incorporate harmonics created by sine waves of varying frequencies and amplitudes.

Chapter 2

Analog and Digital Audio Connections

There's no single connector for analog or digital audio, but there are several common ones—so let's consider the options. First, though, we'll look at how analog signals travel between devices like a microphone output and a mixer input.

Balanced and Unbalanced Lines

With wired connections, the two main ways of transferring signals from one device to another are *unbalanced* and *balanced* lines. They use different types of connectors and cables.

Unbalanced Connections

The common musical instrument cable is an example of an unbalanced line with two conductors. One wire is the *ground* line (also called common, earth, shield, or DC return). The other is the *hot* line, which carries the signal (Fig. 2.1).

Figure 2.1 This 1/4-inch phone plug has two conductors for unbalanced systems. The tip is the hot connection, and the rest of the shaft (the sleeve) is the ground connection.

Almost all guitar processors and amps have an unbalanced input for compatibility with conventional electric guitars and other electrified musical instruments. Unbalanced systems generally use two-wire 1/4-inch phone connectors or RCA phono jacks and plugs (as used in hi-fi gear; see Fig. 2.2).

Figure 2.2 Phono plugs, also called RCA plugs, are unbalanced. They're common in consumer gear as well as some audio equipment.

Balanced Connections

A balanced system adds another signal line (called the *cold* line) to the hot signal-line-plus-ground combination of an unbalanced system (Fig. 2.3). The Tech Talk sidebar below provides technical details, but the benefit is that a balanced line helps reject hum and noise that an unbalanced cable might pick up (e.g., by being close to a power transformer or AC line).

Figure 2.3 This balanced phone plug has three conductors—the Tip (hot or +), the Ring (cold, -, or neutral), and the Sleeve (ground). The first letter of these terms is what gives balanced phone plugs and jacks the abbreviation "TRS" connectors.

Note that unbalanced stereo wiring can use the same type of 1/4-inch phone connector, with the tip being the left signal, the ring being the right signal, and the sleeve being ground. However, the TRS connection for a balanced line carries a balanced mono signal, not an unbalanced stereo signal.

Tech Talk: How Balanced Lines Work

With a balanced line, as an audio signal's voltage increases along one line, its out-of-phase equivalent on the other line decreases. This type of signal has to feed a special type of input, found in audio transformers and certain amplifier designs, that responds to the *difference* between these out-of-phase signals (if the input added the out-of-phase signals together, they'd cancel). This *differential input* rejects signals that spill over into both signal lines equally, such as hum and noise. Because the differential input responds only to the differences between the two signal lines, when the same signal is present on both lines, the differential input ignores them.

Is Balanced Better?

Balanced lines are preferred with long cable runs, especially ones carrying low-signal levels that are subject to noise or interference. In a small studio or onstage setup with relatively short cable runs and high signal levels, unbalanced connections are sufficient—but you'll need to use balanced connections for your mics, because almost all professional mics are designed for balanced-line operation.

Signal Level Categories

Analog audio systems in home studios handle three broad categories of signal levels. Some devices, like a mixer or audio interface, may handle all three, while others may handle only one.

♦ *Mic level* signals have the lowest level of the three, and therefore require amplification to bring them up to line level.

♦ *Line level* is a higher-level signal generated by electronic instruments, mixers, and other devices that don't require additional amplification within the interface itself.

♦ *Instrument-level* signals, associated with electric guitar, bass, and other instruments with *passive pickups,* have a signal strength somewhere between mic and line levels.

Pickups with built-in electronics, like amplifiers, are called *active pickups.*

With line-level analog signals, there are two common nominal levels: +4 dB (a higher signal level that's common in pro setups) and −10 dB (a lower signal level that's used more for home recording). For example, most guitar preamps, synthesizers, and other music gear use −10 dB levels. Pro, large-format mixing consoles use +4 dB levels. You don't really need to know the theory behind this; just note that −10 dB devices are optimized for lower signal levels than +4 dB devices.

The indications +4 and −10, or +4 dB and −10 dB, are commonly used abbreviations for +4 dBu and −10 dBv, respectively.

For more specifics on the decibel, see Chapter 3 of this book.

In theory, connecting +4 and −10 gear together can create a gain mismatch. In practice, today's recording gear is fairly tolerant of different levels. Feeding a −10 output into a +4 input will likely not cause a significant noise increase; likewise, turning down an input control can trim a +4 signal down to −10 levels. Some interfaces have a switch in a software application that optimizes the interface for line-level signals that are either +4 dB or −10 dB (Fig. 2.4).

Figure 2.4 The control panel for Universal Audio's Apollo Twin audio interface has a software switch for selecting an output reference level of either −10 dB or +4 dB.

However, there could also be a mechanical switch that alters these levels (Fig. 2.5).

Figure 2.5 TASCAM's US-20x20 interface has a rear-panel switch to select between nominal −10 dB and +4 dB levels.

Analog Audio Connector Types

Following are the most common types of analog audio connectors.

XLR Connectors

These connect to professional-level microphones and some gear with +4 signal levels; XLR connectors have balanced connections with three pins (Fig. 2.6). The jacks usually indicate the associated pin numbers (1, 2, and 3) because there's a standardized way to wire these: pin 1 is ground, pin 2 is the hot or + connection, and pin 3 is the cold or − connection.

Figure 2.6 The XLR plug on the left plugs into an XLR jack mic input on the right; the label helpfully indicates which pin is ground, hot, and cold.

Tech Talk: Phantom Power

With pro audio gear designed for use with mics, such as mic preamps and mixers, the balanced XLR connection may also carry *phantom power*—a +48V DC voltage needed to power condenser mics (and some ribbon mics with built-in preamps). Most audio interfaces and mixers with XLR jacks can switch on phantom power, which sends power from the XLR jack down the mic cable to the mic. Devices with XLR outputs that aren't microphones should not be subjected to phantom power. Although their outputs will likely be protected against accidentally applying phantom power, this isn't guaranteed.

1/4-Inch Phone Connectors

We covered 1/4-inch phone plugs earlier, now let's look at phone jacks. Although 1/4-inch balanced TRS phone jacks appear to use standard 1/4-inch guitar-cord-type jacks, balanced connections use stereo jacks that are wired for balanced mono operation (instead of being wired for unbalanced stereo). The preceding sections on balanced and unbalanced lines show the types of plugs used with these jacks. Because it's not obvious from looking at the outside of phone jacks whether they're balanced or unbalanced, products will indicate that they're balanced (Fig. 2.7). As shown in Figures 2.5 and 2.6, they may also show which connections are hot, cold, and ground (tip, ring, and sleeve respectively).

Figure 2.7 The line outputs on this PreSonus interface use balanced TRS connections. Most interfaces designed for home recording use 1/4-inch TRS output jacks for balanced lines because there isn't enough room to dedicate XLR jacks for both the inputs and outputs.

Balanced 1/4-inch input connections are compatible with 1/4-inch unbalanced lines because if you use an unbalanced plug, a balanced input simply turns into an unbalanced input. This often works with output connections as well, as long as shorting out the – (cold) balanced line to ground doesn't cause a problem. The unbalanced connection will have half the level of a balanced connection. Also, note that adapters are available to convert XLR connections to balanced 1/4-inch connections, and vice-versa.

Combination Jacks

These space-saving jacks combine an XLR connector with a 1/4-inch TRS connector located inside the XLR section (Fig. 2.8). This universal solution lets you plug in XLR balanced, 1/4-inch balanced, or 1/4-inch unbalanced lines.

Figure 2.8 A combi jack takes up about as much panel space as a standard XLR jack, but you can plug a 1/4-inch phone plug into the center.

1/8-Inch Stereo Mini Connectors

While waning a bit in popularity, you'll find these in some smartphones, extension speakers, MP3 players, and the like. Sometimes they're also used as output jacks designed to feed headphones (Fig. 2.9).

Figure 2.9 An 1/8-inch headphone output jack is on the left, and an 1/8-inch stereo plug is on the right.

If you need a stereo 1/8-inch input or output and have only 1/4-inch connectors, look for 1/4-inch to 1/8-inch adapters, which are readily available.

Digital Audio Connector Types

Now let's consider the most common connectors and signal transfer protocols used for digital audio. Digital hookups are not that different from analog ones—outputs go to inputs. However, these signals run at a higher frequency than standard audio. Fiber-optic cables can handle high frequencies easily, but standard audio cables may not be satisfactory if they distort the waveform by not reproducing rapid signal-level changes properly. This can affect signal transfer, and it's why some cables are designated as being specifically for digital audio.

 Digital-to-digital transfers require no level setting—code is code, so the maximum level (also called "full code") on one device is equivalent to the maximum level on any other digital audio device.

S/PDIF (Sony/Philips Digital Interface)

This is a common digital interface, because S/PDIF outputs are also found in some consumer electronics. S/PDIF carries a stereo digital audio signal, and typically uses either RCA (phono) electrical coaxial connectors (Fig. 2.10) or TOSLINK fiber-optic connectors for input and output connections.

 Trivia time: TOSLINK is short for Toshiba Link, and is a registered trademark of Toshiba. The generic name is EIAJ Optical.

Figure 2.10   Coaxial S/PDIF connections use RCA phono connectors in consumer gear, although some professional equipment uses XLR connectors.

S/PDIF can also use XLR connectors, which are preferred for AES/EBU digital audio signals (described next). However, because S/PDIF and AES/EBU connections have different levels, there's usually a switch to select between the two types of digital audio signals if a piece of gear is designed to handle both.

Tech Talk: How to Make an AES/EBU to S/PDIF Adapter for Wired Connections

Sometimes you may need to interface an AES/EBU port to a S/PDIF port. If so, you can make a cable with an XLR connector (for AES/EBU) at one end and an RCA phono jack at the other end. Connect the XLR's "hot" lead and ground to the phono jack's hot lead and ground, respectively. Although the AES/EBU signal will be stronger than the S/PDIF signal (this has nothing to do with audio level, just electrical characteristics), most of the time the two will interface successfully.

However, when going from AES/EBU output to S/PDIF input, it's good practice to insert a 220-ohm current-limiting resistor in the hot lead to provide a bit of attenuation.

Although optical connectors included for S/PDIF may also work with digital audio signals based on the ADAT optical interface described later, this is not always a given. Most S/PDIF connections are coaxial, although some interfaces use optical TOSLINK connectors for both S/PDIF and ADAT (Fig. 2.11).

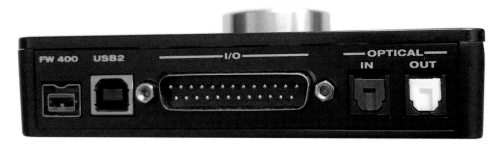

Figure 2.11 MOTU's Track16 interface has TOSLINK input and output optical connectors that are compatible with S/PDIF and the ADAT multichannel optical interface. The 25-pin I/O connector mates with a breakout cable that provides two line inputs, a guitar (instrument) input, two main outs, two line outs, two XLR mic inputs, MIDI in, and MIDI out. This interface also has the unusual feature of offering both FireWire 400 and USB 2.0 ports for computer connections.

AES/EBU (Audio Engineering Society/European Broadcast Union)

This is another two-channel interface that is similar to S/PDIF, but uses balanced, XLR-style connectors and is associated more with pro gear (Fig. 2.12). Some audio interfaces offer both AES/EBU and S/PDIF (optical or coax) connectors.

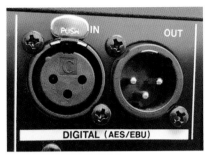

Figure 2.12 Input and output XLR connectors for AES/EBU digital audio connections.

ADAT (Alesis Digital Audio Tape) Optical Interface

This 8-channel interface uses TOSLINK connectors, and sends/receives signals over a fiber-optic cable. While originally used with the Alesis ADAT recorders, over the years it has become a *de facto* multichannel standard—mixers, hard disk recorders, and other devices often include an ADAT connector (Fig. 2.13).

Figure 2.13 Although ADAT digital tape recorders are on the verge of extinction, the ADAT optical connection lives on.

Perhaps the most common, current application of an audio interface's ADAT input is to expand an audio interface's number of input channels. There are 8-channel mic preamps with an ADAT output, which you can connect to your audio interface's ADAT input, and *voilà*—eight extra mic inputs. Compact, desktop-type interfaces with limited inputs often include an ADAT input to allow for easy expansion.

ADAT S/MUX

This is similar to the standard ADAT protocol, but the original spec could not handle sample rates above 48 kHz. The S/MUX protocol *multiplexes* (splits) a higher sample rate signal (88.2 kHz or 96 kHz) between two digital audio streams by sending one sample over one stream, and the next sample over the other stream. So, even though the digital audio streams run at 44.1 or 48 kHz, when demultiplexed, the result is a higher sample rate. The drawback is that ADAT S/MUX can carry only half as many channels of audio as the usual ADAT spec (Fig. 2.14).

Figure 2.14 A pair of ADAT connectors can create the ADAT S/MUX interface for sample rates higher than the original 44.1 kHz / 48 kHz options. The labels on the rear panel of this PreSonus interface show the 16 channel assignments for standard 44.1 / 48 kHz ADAT connections (above the TOSLINK connectors) and the 8 channel assignments for 88.2 / 96 kHz S/MUX assignments (below the connectors).

ADAT S/MUX IV

Another and rarer alternative, S/MUX IV, accommodates two channels of 192 kHz/24-bit audio over a standard ADAT optical cable.

MADI (Multichannel Audio Digital Interface)

Originally designed to transfer 56 channels of audio over coaxial cables, you'll find MADI in higher-end consoles and interfaces. An enhanced version, Extended MADI (also called MADI-X) provides up to 64 channels at 48 kHz and 32 channels at 96 kHz, and can also use optical or Cat 5 cables (Cat 5 cables are the kind used for Ethernet). RME is a company that makes a range of MADI interfaces (Fig. 2.15), but so far MADI is rare in home and project studios.

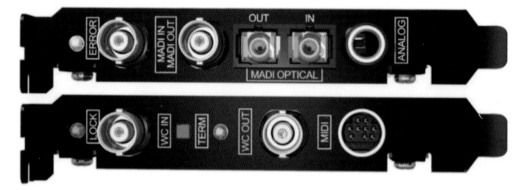

Figure 2.15 The MADI interface can transfer up to 64 audio channels over wire or optical connections. The RME HDSPe interface includes both options.

Computer Audio Connectors

Devices such as audio interfaces, and some other musical gear (instruments, multieffects, and even guitar amps), can transfer digital audio to and from computers over standard computer ports. Unlike analog signal lines, and digital audio connections between dedicated pieces of gear, the audio connections for computers do more than just carry audio—they are typically bi-directional data buses that can carry independent digital audio data streams, as well as provide power to a connected peripheral. Not all computers have connectors for the three main ports, so make *sure* you know what your computer uses so it can communicate with your digital gear.

An important characteristic of all digital computer connections is *speed*—how fast they can transfer data. In practical terms, higher speed connections have two main benefits:

♦ They can handle a greater number of simultaneous audio channels (for example, a live recording where you need to record multiple, independent audio signals).

♦ They have less *latency*. When monitoring a signal through the computer, there can be a noticeable delay called latency. For example, if you're singing a vocal and monitoring the computer's output in your headphones, with higher latencies you'll hear a delay, as if you were singing through an echo unit set to a short echo. With high-speed interfaces, this delay will likely not be objectionable, and may not even be noticeable.

USB (Universal Serial Bus)

This is the most common computer port for digital audio devices, because it gives solid, reliable performance. USB has evolved over the years to become faster and more efficient. Early USB 1.1 interfaces were limited in how many audio channels they could handle. USB 2.0, the next generation, used the same connectors for physical compatibility, but offered a significant speed increase. USB 3.0 added more lines for greater speed, but this altered the connector; however, it remained compatible with USB 2.0 connectors if you were willing to forego the speed increase. USB 3.1 and 3.2 upped the speed even more, and changed the connector (again) to the more universal USB-C type. Fortunately, with suitable adapters, older USB devices can connect to USB-C ports. Figure 2.16 shows common USB connectors.

Figure 2.16   Connectors from left to right: USB Type A, USB Type B, USB Mini B, USB Micro B, USB 3.0, and USB-C.

FireWire (also called IEEE-1394)

This connection protocol is in its twilight years. Although intended originally for use with peripherals like camcorders, FireWire can work well for transferring digital audio between a computer and an external device, like an audio interface. If a Windows computer lacks FireWire, but its motherboard has slots, you can add a FireWire PCIe card to provide multiple FireWire ports. If your computer doesn't have slots, but has a Thunderbolt connection (described next), you can use FireWire audio interfaces with an adapter, although their performance won't match Thunderbolt's.

As with USB, FireWire has evolved over the years. The original FireWire 400 interface had two types of connectors: 4-pin and 6-pin. Aside from size, the main difference is that the 6-pin connector can provide power, as well as carry data, whereas the 4-pin one carries only data. FireWire 800 runs at twice the speed of FireWire 400, and its connector has nine pins (Fig. 2.17).

Figure 2.17 Left to right: Four-pin and six-pin FireWire 400 connectors, and a FireWire 800 connector. Some FireWire 400 systems use the FireWire 800 connector.

Thunderbolt

Apple computers are most commonly associated with Thunderbolt ports, although they're starting to have more of a presence on Windows machines. Thunderbolt 3 is the latest version and offers several advantages over previous generations (as well as over other interface protocols), including higher speed. Adapters are also available for devices using FireWire, PCIe cards, earlier versions of USB, and other protocols, for compatibility with Thunderbolt ports. Thunderbolt 3 is backwards compatible with almost all older Thunderbolt peripherals. Thunderbolt 3 peripherals may be compatible with Thunderbolt 1 or 2 ports.

Before investing in a Thunderbolt interface, *make sure your computer is compatible.* The interface manufacturer's web site will likely provide information on compatibility. For example, an interface may be supported starting with a particular processor generation or Thunderbolt 3 controller chip, but may not have been tested with previous generations. Just because something isn't *officially* supported doesn't mean it won't work, but you'll be taking an expensive chance.

Thunderbolt 3 uses the same USB-C connector as USB 3.1, and a Thunderbolt port is compatible with USB 3.1 peripherals. (However, the reverse isn't true—you can't hook up a Thunderbolt peripheral to a USB 3.1 port.) The first two generations of Thunderbolt used different connectors, and were not natively compatible with USB (Fig. 2.18).

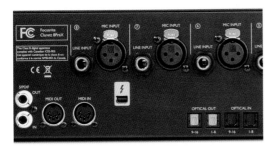

Figure 2.18 Thunderbolt 1 and 2 used a different connector compared to Thunderbolt 3's USB-C connector. Focusrite's Clarett 8PreX groups the Thunderbolt port with other digital connectors (S/PDIF, MIDI, and optical).

Key Takeaways

♦ Unbalanced connections are more common with musical instruments and home studios, and almost always use 1/4-inch phone and RCA phono connectors.

♦ 1/8-inch unbalanced stereo mini connectors are common with many smartphones, portable audio players, and the like. You may also find them on products designed for mobile use.

♦ Balanced connections are associated with pro studios and usually employ XLR or TRS 1/4-inch jacks.

♦ Don't fret too much about +4 dB and −10 dB levels, or balanced and unbalanced lines, unless you have a big studio with long cable runs. Use whatever works.

♦ Combi jacks are great because they accommodate 1/4-inch balanced or unbalanced plugs, as well as XLR plugs.

♦ S/PDIF is often available on modern consumer gear, but in today's studio, there's not a lot of need for stereo digital audio transfers.

♦ S/PDIF connectors are either wired and use RCA phono connectors, or optical and use TOSLINK connectors.

♦ Even though the original ADAT tape machines are legacy devices, the ADAT optical connector is still used to interconnect mixers, audio interfaces, and multi-channel mic preamps.

♦ MADI and MADI-X are multichannel digital audio interface protocols that can transfer up to 64 audio channels over wire or optical connectors.

♦ Digital audio can travel over computer connections like USB, FireWire, and Thunderbolt.

♦ USB is the most popular port option for computer audio, FireWire is fading, and Thunderbolt is common on newer Macs, but not yet commonplace with Windows.

Chapter 3

Measuring and Specifying Audio

It's important to be able to quantify audio characteristics and performance. When evaluating gear, it helps to know the gear's specifications so you can make an informed judgment as to what might be best for your needs. When recording, you need to know signal levels so you can avoid sending in a signal that is too high or too low for your recording system.

Before digital technology, tools to measure audio were expensive and difficult to calibrate. Meters had limited display capabilities. Today's software offers sophisticated measuring and analysis tools that can help us better understand how audio behaves in a system.

Measuring Audio

Analytic tools to see amplitude and frequency are an essential part of the recording process. Part of their value is in training our ears—a visual representation of what we hear can help us learn to recognize different levels and frequencies solely with our ears. Audio measurement tools range from the simple to the complex; we'll look at the more common ones.

Tech Talk: Listening with Your Eyes—Pros and Cons

You'll often hear advice not to "listen with your eyes." This is to emphasize that ultimately, your ears need to judge whether something sounds right. For example, if you fix all pitches in a vocal so they're all perfectly in tune, they may *look* right—but they may not *sound* right. However, being able to quantify what you're hearing will educate your ears. Before digital delays, I wasn't really sure how long a 50 ms delay lasted. Being able to see the delay time in a readout helped educate my ears. As a result, I can now dial in the right amount of delay much faster, because I know what to expect for specific delay times.

Level Meters

Level meters are an important part of hardware and software audio devices, because the meters relate signal levels to *dynamic range*—the difference between the highest and lowest signal levels an audio stage can resolve. Levels that exceed the dynamic range create distortion. Residual noise masks excessively low levels, causing them to no longer be measurable or perceivable.

Level meters can indicate whether we're feeding in too little level, too much level, or level that's optimum for the system's dynamic range.

Generally, meters measure levels in one of two ways:

- **Peak.** The meter shows a signal's instantaneous peak level. If your priority is making sure a signal doesn't clip and cause distortion, peak is the most useful response.

- **RMS.** The meter displays an average signal level. Long, sustained sounds register higher on the meter than short, percussive sounds, and meter movement is slower. An RMS level indication correlates more closely with how our ears perceive level.

Modern Level Metering

Old-school, mechanical meters with a moving needle and calibrated scale (which shows average levels, not peaks) are primitive in what they can display. Digital technology has changed that, from the virtual meters in a program's virtual console, to the hardware meters that use displays based on newer technologies like OLEDs (Organic Light-Emitting Diodes). Today's meters may have some, or even all of the following parameters (shown in Fig. 3.1):

- **Ballistics.** This determines whether the response is "snappy" or slow, by altering the rate at which the meter refreshes its readings. Faster rates give a quicker response, but stress your CPU a bit more than slower refresh rates. With today's fast CPUs, that shouldn't be an issue. However, faster rates are visually more "jittery," so you might want to slow down the rate anyway.

- **Peak hold and decay times**. Peak hold maintains the highest peak value for a specified amount of time. This could be a few seconds, or it could persist until reset. The reason for this is so that if you miss seeing a peak because you were looking elsewhere, you can still know the value of the highest peak that occurred. Decay time sets the time for a meter to return to zero after the signal stops.

 You can set a short decay time (around 100 ms) to determine which tracks have effects tails due to time-based effects. After pressing a transport's Stop button, the meters for tracks with delay or reverb will show a level reading longer than the other tracks.

- **Meter Range.** Different meter ranges can optimize a meter for the task at hand. If you choose the maximum dynamic range (e.g., 90 dB), you can see low-level signals (like hiss or hum) creeping into the recording. For playback, a 48 dB range is a good balance between focusing on what's happening at higher levels but not missing lower-level signals. For dance music or high-intensity rock, a 12 or 24 dB range can show whether there's plenty of activity at higher levels.

- **Peak + RMS.** This type of meter shows both peak and RMS values. For example, the RMS value might be a bar graph, and the peak a different-colored bar that floats over it.

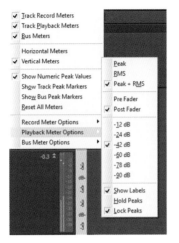

Figure 3.1 The meters in Cakewalk by BandLab include options for Peak, RMS, or Peak + RMS (the orange dots toward the top of the meter indicate the last attained peak), as well as meter range and the ability to show a numeric label for the peak level (−0.3 in the picture).

Spectrum Analyzers

A spectrum analyzer shows the level at different frequencies. It does this by dividing the audible frequency spectrum into hundreds, or even thousands of bands (also called *windows)* using a process called Fast Fourier Transform (FFT). It then displays the level of each band in a graph or 3D display.

This feedback is invaluable for correlating what you *hear* to data you *see* about frequency response and amplitude. Most digital audio editing programs and even some multitrack hosts (Fig. 3.2) now include software spectrum analysis tools.

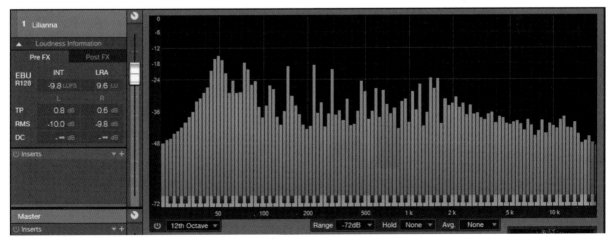

Figure 3.2 The Project page in Studio One Pro, which is designed for mastering, includes a spectrum analyzer to show the amplitude in various frequency bands. Each band represents 1/12th of an octave, and the range is set to −72 dB (maximum is −144 dB). The numbers toward the left measure loudness, peak, and average values.

The goal is not to try for a flat response across the spectrum. Generally, the highs trail off gently, while what happens in the bass depends on the musical genre. For example, you'll see more bass on a dance mix with a prominent kick drum. A very uneven average bass response may indicate acoustics-related problems—either from room resonances when miking acoustic sources, or from mixing if EQ was used to compensate for room anomalies of which you're not aware.

Spectrum analyzers are also helpful for analyzing the spectral response of well-mixed, well-mastered recordings. Compare their curves to your music. Differences are not necessarily a problem; it depends on the music and style. But if your mixes sound too muddy, too bright, or otherwise lack clarity in comparison to commercially available music, observe the dissimilarities across the audio spectrum to see if any areas need compensation to be louder or softer. Of course, you can determine this just by listening—but a spectrum analyzer can point you toward potential problem areas quickly.

Different programs offer different spectrum analyzer features. Some programs take (or even save) "snapshots," some take an average reading over time, and some can "fly out" the display to show more detail. A few programs can compare the input and output spectrum in relation to a signal processing function.

Regardless of a spectrum analyzer's specifics, when used for purposes beyond "eye candy," they can present useful information—especially about mixes. With practice, someday you'll probably be able to say, "This mix needs a slight boost at 12 kHz, a major cut around 350 Hz, and a minor notch at 50 Hz." Until then, you can use spectrum analysis to display this information visually, so you can learn more about your mixes.

Tech Talk: Customizing Spectrum Analysis Response

Some programs can customize the way a spectrum analyzer displays data, as well as alter its analysis process, with some or all of the following options (see Fig. 3.3):

- **FFT size** determines the number of samples per band. Higher numbers give better frequency resolution, but require more time to compute the display. When you're looking for frequency anomalies, use a high value, like 16K or 32K. This catches very narrow peaks that you might not see with smaller FFT sizes.

- **FFT overlap** sets the amount by which the analysis bands overlap. Higher values (50% and above) provide a more accurate analysis, but increase display computation time.

- **Smoothing window** determines the analysis algorithm. Different algorithms trade off sharper, more distinct peaks for *leakage* between neighboring bands (i.e., data in one band will influence the ones next to it). A Triangular smoothing window is a compromise between peak sharpness and leakage. Rectangular provides accurate drawing of peaks with high leakage, while Blackman-Harris has little leakage, with peaks that look more rounded.

- **3D vs. 2D** shows the information in different ways. 2D shows amplitude versus frequency, while 3D displays a series of "slices" within the selected region to relate time to frequency and amplitude.

- **Range, reference,** etc. are parameters for adjusting the scale, zooming in on specific areas of the graph, changing the 0 dB reference point, etc.

- **Linear vs. log response** is best set to Log for audio work, because the curve more closely approximates how your hearing responds.

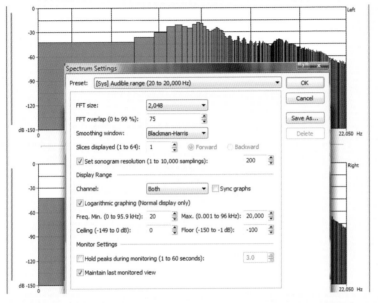

Figure 3.3 Magix Sound Forge provides multiple customization options for its spectrum analyzer display.

Phase and Correlation Meters

These meters, which check stereo/mono compatibility and other playback characteristics, are often incorporated in the same display. The phase meter, also called a goniometer, shows how a stereo signal's left and right channels occupy the stereo field.

 Goniometers are invaluable for surround sound, but that application is beyond the scope of this book.

The phase meter's main use is for diagnostic purposes. A mono signal appears as a straight, vertical line down the display's center. A straight line on the L or R axis indicates that there's signal in only that channel (left or right). The wider the stereo effect, the more the display extends toward the right and left (Fig. 3.4); the vertical size indicates level.

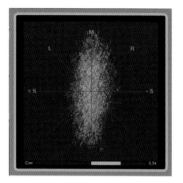

Figure 3.4 The phase meter shows that this signal is neither mono nor super-wide stereo, but somewhere in between. The correlation meter's bar graph is on the bottom.

If the signal tends toward the left (or right) *and* the middle, then it's mid-side encoded—a recording technique that's covered in other books in this series, including *Microphones for the Recording Musician.*

Phase meters aren't only for checking final mixes. For insight into the phase, level, and stereo spread of individual tracks, insert a phase meter in the master output bus, then solo one track at a time. A program's *exclusive* solo function, where engaging a solo button mutes all other tracks, can make this easier.

The correlation meter (the bar graph at the phase meter's bottom in Fig. 3.4) indicates a stereo signal's mono compatibility. This was crucial when mastering for vinyl, because it could indicate if out-of-phase audio components could possibly cause the stylus to jump out of its groove.

Although stereo is now dominant, it's still important to check for mono compatibility because listening over speakers combines signals into mono to some extent. You'll usually monitor correlation in the master bus, but for individual tracks, a correlation meter can indicate whether (for example) a signal processor is throwing a track's left and right channels out of phase.

A correlation meter's reading ranges from −1 (the right and left channels are completely out of phase, with no correlation) to +1 (the right and left channels are identical). With most mixes, the bar graph will fluctuate between 0 and +1. If the correlation meter shows a negative number, then there are out-of-phase elements within the stereo mix. Occasional negative excursions aren't a problem, but if the correlation meter spends a substantial amount of time in negative territory, then there's a phase issue that will interfere with mono compatibility.

Real-Time Analyzers

These are sophisticated measuring tools that can analyze a variety of audio characteristics—frequency response, distortion, and the like. The later section on Common Audio Specifications includes several examples of how they work.

Understanding Audio Specifications

Specifications can help us understand performance similarities and differences among various pieces of gear; unfortunately, though, many manufacturer spec sheets are meaningless, because they don't provide the conditions under which the tests were performed. For example, measuring a preamp's noise level with the gain turned up full yields less impressive specs than if the preamp's gain is turned down all the way.

Results can also depend on the reference level—for a given amount of noise, measuring signal-to-noise ratio by comparing the maximum possible output level to the residual noise will seem much better than a spec that compares the noise to a reference level that's lower than the maximum possible output. Nonetheless, specifications at least make generalizations about different pieces of gear.

 Always use specs as a guide, not a judge. If you'd like to know why it's difficult to make objective gear comparisons from manufacturer spec sheets, Rane has published a deep, and forthright, explanation of specifications available here: http://www.rane.com/note145.html.

The Problem with Ears

Even healthy, young ears aren't perfect. The ear has a midrange peak and does not respond as well to low and high frequencies, particularly at lower volumes. The response comes closest to a flat response at relatively high levels. The Fletcher-Munson curve (Fig. 3.5) illustrates this phenomenon.

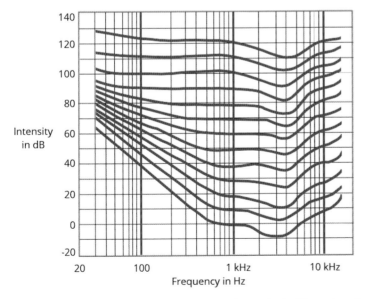

Figure 3.5 The Fletcher-Munson curve shows that different parts of the audio spectrum need to be at different levels to be perceived as having the same volume. Low frequencies have to be substantially louder at lower levels to be perceived as having equal volume.

Your ears' limitations become more pronounced if you don't take care of your hearing (e.g., listen to loud music for prolonged periods of time, do deep sea diving, drink a lot of alcohol, etc.). Even flying can affect your ears' high frequency response. I wait at least 24 hours after flying before mixing or mastering; the few times I've disregarded that rule, mixes that seemed fine played back too bright the next day. And no matter how well you take care of your hearing, age will take its toll.

It's crucial to care for your hearing. In my touring days when I'd often play 200 days out of the year, I wore cotton in my ears. While not as effective as present-day earplugs, I feel it saved my hearing. I often carry the cylindrical foam ear plugs available at sporting good stores and wear them while walking on city streets, at clubs, when hammering or using power tools, or anywhere my ears will get more abuse than people talking at a conversational level. Please prioritize taking care of your ears.

 Schedule an appointment with an audiologist at least once every year or two. Some hearing issues that lead to deafness can be prevented if caught in time. Wax buildup can also be a problem; an ear, nose, and throat doctor can remove it safely.

Frequency Response, Hearing, and the Decibel

Human ears are the most universal piece of "audio equipment." If the ear was a perfect listening machine, and if a sound source (loudspeaker or whatever) produced tones from 20 Hz to 20 kHz at exactly the same level, then the high-frequency tones would sound just as loud as the low-frequency ones. This would be an example of *flat response*—i.e., the response would be consistent throughout the audible frequency range. But because ears are imperfect, we have to deal with a deviation from flat response. What's more, there are additional trouble spots in the audio signal chain.

A speaker never has a flat frequency response. No matter how much you spend, every speaker will deviate to some degree from an ideal response. For example, at very high frequencies, a loudspeaker has to create very fast air pressure variations—but the mass of the speaker's cone, friction, and other error sources make accurate high-frequency reproduction difficult. At the other end of the audio range, even a 12-inch speaker can have trouble moving enough air to generate the massive air pressure changes required by low notes, which affects the low frequency response.

A typical loudspeaker's frequency response rolls off toward both the extreme high and low ends, but that's not all: *resonances* (response anomalies) in the speaker and speaker enclosure itself can cause response deviations. To complicate matters further, the room in which you listen to the speaker will also change the response. A room with many hard surfaces (concrete, glass, etc.) will bounce high frequencies around and make them appear more prominent, while a thickly carpeted room will absorb many of the high frequencies. And we're not done yet... headphones, microphones, and other transducers that convert mechanical energy to electrical energy also introduce their own deviations.

Amplifiers don't have perfect frequency responses either, but compared to our ears (or loudspeakers), they're excellent. Many amplifiers can reproduce tones from 20 Hz to 20 kHz, or even 100 kHz, with ruler-flat response. Generally, the amp will not be the weak link in an audio system. They can even improve the sound—with powered monitor speakers, the accompanying amps are often designed to compensate for frequency response variations in the speakers themselves.

Why Flat Response Is Good

We're reaching the moral of the story: with so many variables between the sound source and the listener, we need to minimize the chaos. Hence, whenever possible, the goal is audio systems with the flattest possible frequency response. Then, the only variables left are the listener's ears, gear, and acoustic environment.

Professional recording studios depend on accurate monitor speakers and acoustically treated rooms to provide the flattest possible frequency response. A listener will hear what the recording engineer heard while mixing if the listener's playback system also has a flat frequency response. But if the studio loudspeaker exaggerates the high frequencies, unless the engineer is aware of this issue, then the highs will likely be mixed at a lower level to compensate. So, any recordings made at that studio will probably lack high frequency response when played over a system with a truly flat response.

For the best audio experience, both the recording and playback systems need to have a flat frequency response. However, because you have no control over the playback system at the listener's end, a flat recording system becomes even more important.

The Decibel

There are several different kinds of decibel (dB), and a complete treatment of this specification could take up a book—so let's deal with the dB in general terms. Reduced to essentials, the dB is a unit of *ratio* between the level of two audio signals. Probably the best way to become familiar with the dB is through examples.

Suppose we're listening to an amplifier/speaker combination and have a sound-level meter calibrated in dB that registers changes in the system's acoustic output. Furthermore, suppose the input to the amplifier is not a complex musical source (such as a recording), but instead is a pure audio test tone that can vary in frequency from 20 Hz to 20 kHz.

Because the dB expresses a ratio, to derive a ratio requires a standard signal to which we can compare other signals. For example, you could adjust a tone generator's output for a comfortable listening level, and adjust a sound-level meter so that it reads "0 dB" at this reference level. Notice that already there's a big advantage to working with the dB: the absolute sound level coming out of the speakers is not important, so we can listen at any volume level. What we're looking for are changes in volume level compared to the standard reference signal. The amount of change—the ratio—is then expressed in dB. A signal that's stronger than the reference creates a ratio that is + (plus) a certain number of dB, while a signal that's weaker than the reference creates a ratio that is − (minus) a certain number of dB.

1 kHz is a common reference frequency, because as mentioned earlier, the greatest response anomalies occur at the limits of the audio spectrum. So, we have a reference frequency (1 kHz) and level (0 dB). Now, let's vary the test tone frequency while monitoring the amplifier/speaker combination's output with the sound level meter. Because no speaker is perfect, the output will vary somewhat at different frequencies. At lower frequencies (below around 70 Hz), the response will start dropping off and become more uneven.

A speaker's response might be summarized as varying no more than 6 dB from 60 Hz up to 18 kHz. A spec sheet would indicate the response as "plus or minus 3 dB, 60 Hz to 18 kHz." This response would be typical of a medium-size, consumer-oriented speaker.

Knowing the speaker's response is important to obtain the most accurate sound from our monitoring system. For example, if we know where the speaker isn't flat, adding equalization can—within reason— flatten out the speaker's response to produce a more accurate monitoring system that helps compensate for frequency response deviations.

We often take devices such as loudspeakers for granted and assume they're accurate. However, even if the speaker is accurate, we still have to deal with room acoustics. As a result, professional recording engineers often "learn" the speakers and room they're using. For example, if you know your monitoring setup has a weaker-than-ideal bass response, you'll learn to be conservative with the amount of bass, knowing that it will sound correct on flatter systems.

Tech Talk: What About Those Different Types of Decibels?

You'll often see dB with a suffix, like dBv, dBu, dBFS, dBA, dBSPL, dBm, dBov, dBO, and dBW (as well as some others I probably don't know about). These usually relate to specific reference levels, and you don't need to know what they mean to record a great vocal. However, for those of you who are curious, the two variations you'll most likely find in analog audio gear are dBV and dBu. dBV assumes that the 0 dB reference is a 1.0-volt RMS audio signal. dBu assumes that the 0 dB reference is a 0.7746-volt RMS signal.

Technically speaking, the −10 dB level we've mentioned previously is −10 dBV, or 0.316 volts RMS (equivalent to −7.78 dBu), while +4 dBu is 1.228 volts RMS. Also note that none of this is really relevant to digital audio levels; for that we have dBFS (Full Scale), where 0 dBFS is the maximum possible level of a digital audio file.

Confused? Don't be. Just write a great song and record it... unless you plan to become an electronics engineer and design gear. Then you'll need to know all these details.

Common Audio Specifications

Ideally, audio gear designed for maximum accuracy should reproduce all audible frequencies equally—bass shouldn't be louder than treble, and vice-versa. A frequency response graph measures the results if you feed test frequencies with the same level into a device's input, then compare whether the output shows any variations. An ideal response would be flat (even) from 20 Hz to 20 kHz, because that's the audible range for humans with good hearing. It's harder to reproduce extremely high or extremely low frequencies.

Figure 3.6 shows a typical audio interface's frequency response graph. This illustration was created by sweeping a constant-level signal from 20 Hz to 20 kHz, then using analysis software to measure the resulting output and display it on a graph.

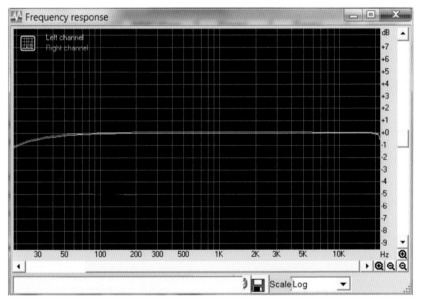

Figure 3.6 This frequency response specification for an audio interface shows that the response has essentially no response deviations from 50 Hz to 20 kHz, and is down 1 dB at 20 Hz. Amplifiers and preamplifiers, the main components in an audio interface, are the most likely studio components to have a truly flat response.

A manufacturer's specification will give a frequency range and amount of response deviation. For example, the spec for the interface shown in the above screenshot could be expressed as –1 dB, +0 dB from 20 Hz to 20 kHz, or ±0.5 dB from 20 Hz to 20 kHz. However, note that specs tend to present products in the best possible light.

Two speakers could have identical printed specs (such as ±3 dB, 50 Hz to 18 kHz), but one could have a much smoother response that just drops off a bit at the extreme high and low frequencies, while the other looks like a relief map of the Alps and has multiple midrange peaks and dips that affect the sound.

Signal-to-Noise Ratio

All electronic devices generate some noise. High-gain circuits (e.g., microphone preamps) generate the most noise, and noise increases with increased gain. For example, here's an audio interface's mic preamp noise level with the volume turned up a fifth of the way (Fig. 3.7).

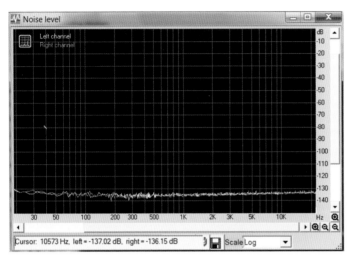

Figure 3.7 The noise is less than −130 dB—in other words, compared to the maximum signal level the interface can handle, the noise is over 130 dB softer.

This graph shows that the signal-to-noise ratio (in this case, the ratio of the full-level signal to the noise) is 130 dB, which is very good. But if we turn up the mic preamp gain two-thirds of the way—about right for recording a quiet vocalist—now the noise level is under −110 dB (Fig. 3.8).

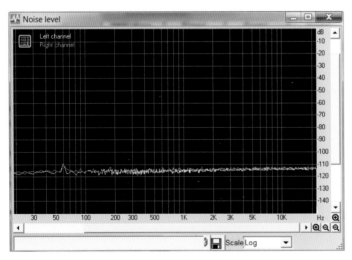

Figure 3.8 Even with the gain turned up, this is still quiet. Consider that a compact disc at its theoretical best can't reproduce levels lower than around −96 dB—essentially, the noise is so low a CD can't reproduce it.

These two graphs also hint that specs have the potential to mislead rather than enlighten. Company "A" might use a graph like Figure 3.7 for their marketing, while Company "B" might choose a more real-world graph like Figure 3.8. Company "A" could imply their mic preamp is quieter—"just look at the specs!" So it's important to know the precise conditions under which specs are measured, which usually aren't given (and to be fair, most people wouldn't know how to interpret them anyway). In this chapter, several of the screenshots for the specs reflect both ideal and real-world conditions.

Noise specs are measured in different ways, so be careful to compare the same kind of spec. The noise spec may be given as EIN (Equivalent Input Noise), which represents the amount of noise a mic preamp adds to a microphone's signal. Lower numbers are better. These numbers are very small, which make the preamps look good.

Another option is *signal-to-noise ratio,* which compares the ratio of a specific level signal (usually for a given, low level of distortion, or the maximum available headroom) to the residual noise. For example, a signal-to-noise ratio of 90 dB means the maximum signal is 90 dB louder than the residual noise.

The noise spec may have a particular *weighting.* This means the spec excludes noise that is less relevant to our hearing, which is perhaps more realistic—but conveniently for manufacturers, it also makes the spec look better. Another noise-related spec, *dynamic range,* is the ratio of the maximum possible level to the minimum level a system can resolve.

With today's equipment, the signal-to-noise ratio usually reflects price. In other words, the noise levels of a particular $400 mic preamp won't differ that much from another $400 mic preamp.

Total Harmonic Distortion

Just as all circuits generate some hiss, they also generate distortion. Distortion means that a waveform has been altered in a way that's usually perceived as undesirable. There are different types of distortion. For example, *hard clipping* distortion means that a signal is undistorted until it exceeds a system's available headroom, at which point the waveform's top and bottom are clipped, and no longer accurately reflect the waveform (Fig. 3.9).

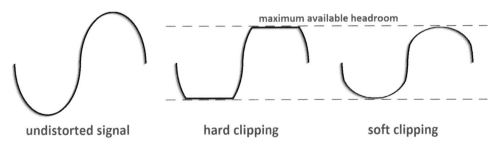

Figure 3.9 Hard clipping cuts off the waveform, which produces a harsh sound. Soft clipping rounds off a waveform that exceeds the available dynamic range, which gives smoother-sounding distortion.

With *soft clipping*, the distortion increases as the waveform starts to approach the maximum available headroom. The distortion doesn't sound as harsh as hard clipping, and is characteristic of the way tubes distort (and as all guitarists know, tube distortion can sound pretty cool).

Total Harmonic Distortion graphs show the level of the harmonics generated by distortion. The standard test feeds in a 1 kHz signal at maximum level. In theory, the output should consist only of that 1 kHz signal. Any other signals represent distortion (Fig. 3.10).

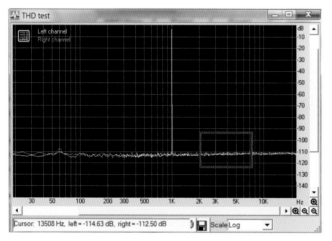

Figure 3.10   The graph shows a little bit of 3rd harmonic distortion at 3 kHz and 5th harmonic distortion at 5 kHz. Both are below −100 dB.

There's additional harmonic distortion not visible in the graph, because it's masked by the noise. Turning the gain all the way down to minimize noise reveals these additional distortion components (Fig. 3.11).

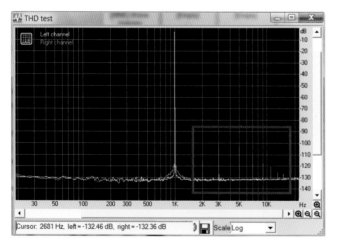

Figure 3.11   With the preamp gain all the way down, the distortion components at 2 kHz, as well as at 7 kHz and above, also become visible above the noise.

Intermodulation Distortion

This type of distortion occurs when two signals interact with each other and produce *artifacts* (undesired sounds not present in the original signals). These artifacts also represent distortion, and many people consider intermodulation distortion more objectionable than harmonic distortion. The standard version of this test feeds in two signals at maximum level, one at 60 Hz and one at 7 kHz. Any output signals other than these two frequencies represent an interaction between the signals, which results in distortion (Fig. 3.12).

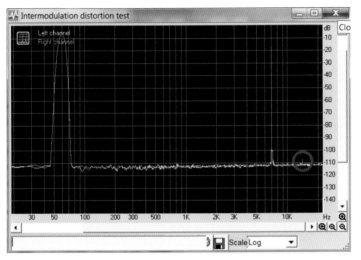

Figure 3.12 The intermodulation distortion is so low it's very difficult to see on this graph. But if you look closely, you'll see a little spike (circled in red) poking up from the noise.

Reducing preamp gain reduces the noise floor, which reveals more distortion artifacts (Fig. 3.13).

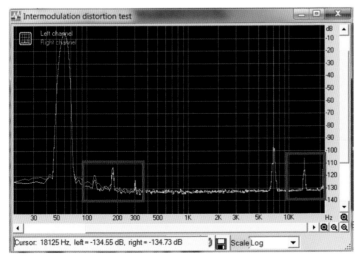

Figure 3.13 With no gain, you can see the four additional low-level distortion components below –110 dB.

Crosstalk

Crosstalk occurs when one channel picks up some signal from another channel. This happens because some components radiate signals, while other components can pick up those signals. Careful mechanical design and signal isolation can reduce crosstalk.

Crosstalk (Fig. 3.14) is more likely with high gain settings at high frequencies, and sometimes, very low frequencies.

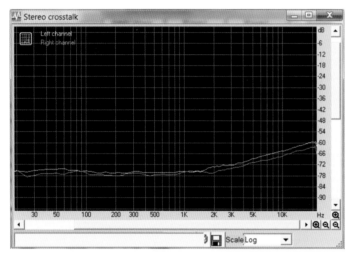

Figure 3.14 This crosstalk spec, taken with a high gain setting, is typical for budget audio interfaces.

When you turn down the gain to a level suitable for recording an instrument like steel-string guitar, crosstalk goes way down (Fig. 3.15).

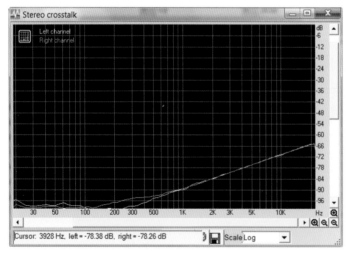

Figure 3.15 Lowering the gain reduces crosstalk considerably.

Tech Talk: Does Digital Audio Narrow the Soundstage?

Some people feel that digital audio doesn't have as wide a soundstage (i.e., stereo spread) as analog audio. This can happen for two reasons. One is crosstalk, where low-level signals spill over from one channel to the other, making the sound more mono. The other is that analog circuits can have more variations than digital audio due to component tolerances. The more dissimilar the left and right channels, the more "stereo" they'll sound.

Key Takeaways

- ◆ Level meters indicate where the signal level falls within a given dynamic range. They can indicate peak and/or average signal levels.

- ◆ Today's software-based digital meters offer far more useful and precise analytical capabilities than the mechanical, moving-needle meters of yesteryear.

- ◆ Spectrum analyzers show signal levels in various frequency bands, and are helpful for analyzing mixes.

- ◆ Phase meters indicate whether a signal is stereo, mono, encoded as a mid-side signal, or has energy exclusively in the left or right channels. They also show the stereo field's width and level.

- ◆ The Correlation meter indicates a stereo signal's mono compatibility.

- ◆ The human ear has response issues that need to be taken into account, especially if your hearing has been abused by constant exposure to loud sounds.

- ◆ The decibel is a unit of measurement that indicates the ratio between two audio signals.

- ◆ Real-time analyzers can provide a graphical display of frequency response, distortion, crosstalk, and other key audio parameters.

- ◆ Use specifications to guide, not to judge. There are many ways to measure specifications, so when comparing the specs for various units, make sure they're all being tested in the same way.

Chapter 4

Digital Audio Sample Rates

When recording audio, after choosing a project's sample rate and *bit resolution*, it's good practice not to change these as you go through the recording, editing, and mixing processes.

 See Chapter 5 of this book for information about bit resolution.

Although it's possible to convert sample rates and bit resolutions, this process usually happens during the last step of the mixing process *if* you need to export your mix to a particular playback medium (e.g., you need to create a CD, but you recorded and mixed at a higher sample rate than a CD's native sample rate). Also note that your sample rate and resolution need to be compatible with your audio interface. Not all audio interfaces support all sample rates or resolutions.

Understanding and Choosing Sample Rates

The sample rate, controlled by a highly accurate and stable system clock, is one of the most important characteristics of a digital audio system. *CD-quality* audio measures the incoming voltage 44,100 times per second (a 44.1 kHz sample rate), which allows the system to reproduce frequencies in the audio range (20 Hz to 20 kHz).

Other common sample rates include:

♦ **Lower than 32 kHz.** These sample rates can't create quality audio. A typical electronic greeting card or toy will have a sample rate below 32 kHz.

♦ **32 kHz.** This is common in digital broadcasting and many satellite transmissions.

♦ **44.1 kHz.** Most home recording projects use this sample rate because it's the "sweet spot" between good fidelity and computer performance.

♦ **48 kHz.** Although not prevalent for audio-only projects, video projects often use 48 kHz for the audio stream. Some recording engineers think 48 kHz sounds better than 44.1 kHz, but any difference is subtle at best.

- **88.2 kHz.** Some people claim this sounds better than 44.1 kHz, while others don't hear a difference. 88.2 kHz is much less common than 96 kHz.

- **96 kHz.** This is the most universal *high-resolution* sample rate. It's common in DVDs and other high-end audio recording processes. Like 88.2 kHz, if you can hear a difference and your gear is up to the task, there's no harm in using higher sample rates (although there can be drawbacks, as described later), and there are even situations (see next) where they can make an audible improvement.

- **176.4 kHz, 192 kHz,** and **384 kHz.** Although some audiophiles believe audio sampled at these rates sounds better than audio at 44.1 kHz or even 96 kHz, these ultra-high sample rates require extra storage and stress out computers more, so they're not used much for multitrack recording projects.

    Currently, the main application for ultra-high sample rates is stereo live recordings of symphony orchestras, classical ensembles, jazz combos, or solo acoustic instruments.

The "High-Resolution" Sample Rate Controversy

There's an ongoing debate among audiophiles, audio engineers, and musicians about whether sample rates higher than 44.1 kHz yield a significant sonic improvement. Theoretically, higher sample rates aren't necessary. Still, some people insist higher sample rates sound better.

The question is whether this is based in fact, or more like a scene from the comedy movie "This Is Spinal Tap," where lead guitarist Nigel Tufnel insists that his amp with knobs that go up to 11 *has* to be better than traditional amps whose knobs only go to 10.

I've recorded many projects at both 44.1 kHz and 96 kHz. With audio *recorded* at 96 kHz, no one has been consistently able to tell the difference between that audio being *played back* at 96 kHz or 44.1 kHz.

However, there can be an audible difference between audio *recorded* at 44.1 kHz or 96 kHz if plug-in software like virtual instruments or amp sims generate sounds *inside* the computer, as opposed to sounds that enter into the computer via an audio interface. Without getting too technical, if a signal source like a virtual instrument generates harmonics that are higher than the project's sampling frequency (i.e., it violates the Nyquist Theorem described in the Tech Talk sidebar), a particular type of distortion can result.

This doesn't happen when recording audio that feeds into an audio interface, because the interface has filters that prevent these harmonics from entering the computer. Sounds generated inside the computer are a different story.

Tech Talk: The Nyquist Theorem

Those who say 44.1 kHz is all you need cite the Nyquist Theorem, which states that a digital system can represent audio accurately at frequencies lower than half the sampling rate (called the Nyquist Limit—e.g., 22.05 kHz in a project with a 44.1 kHz sample rate). Another way to say this is that the sampling frequency needs to be at least twice as high as the highest frequency you need to sample, including harmonic frequencies. Therefore, since humans can't hear much above 20 kHz (and even hearing that high is rare in adults), it certainly seems reasonable that a 44.1 kHz sample rate would suffice.

However, those who contend you need a higher frequency believe the Nyquist Theorem overlooks factors that could make a difference—like an analog-to-digital converter that's optimized to run at 96 kHz, and therefore sounds better at that sample rate. Also, in some situations signals can exceed the Nyquist frequency, which requires raising the sample rate to be in conformance with the Nyquist Theorem.

For example, pulse waves from a plug-in virtual instrument (like a synthesizer) can generate harmonics that extend higher than the pulse wave's fundamental frequency. So can harmonics created by a high-gain amp sim. If steps aren't taken within the plug-in to remove these frequencies, or place a high-frequency limit on them, they may be higher than the Nyquist frequency. This creates a type of distortion known as *foldover distortion* or *aliasing*.

Consider a virtual instrument plug-in that generates harmonic content above the Nyquist Limit—for example, a harmonic at 40 kHz with a 44.1 kHz project. You won't hear a 40 kHz tone, but you will hear the aliasing created when this tone "folds down" (to 4.1 kHz, in this case) below the clock frequency. Aliasing thus appears within the audible range, but is harmonically unrelated to the original signal, and generally sounds pretty ugly.

Avoiding Foldover Distortion

Fortunately, foldover distortion isn't a common problem; it occurs mostly with older virtual instruments and amp sim plug-ins. You could probably go through your entire musical career being blissfully unaware of this issue, and it would not make your music any less effective. Besides, not all plug-ins exhibit foldover distortion, for one of four reasons:

- The audio doesn't generate frequencies high enough to interfere with the project's sample rate frequency.

- The plug-in or the host itself can *oversample* internally (see the Tech Talk sidebar for more about oversampling). This means that as far as the plug-in is concerned, the sample rate is higher than that of the project. So, any foldover distortion occurs outside the audio range.

♦ The project sample rate is high enough to provide the same kind of environment as oversampling.

♦ The plug-in designers have included appropriate anti-alias filtering.

Tech Talk: Oversampling vs. Upsampling

This is a preemptive strike against a flood of internet comments saying, "You don't know the difference between oversampling and upsampling." There are semi-standard definitions for both.

Oversampling generally relates to hardware (for example A/D and D/A converters), and refers to using a sample rate that's some factor higher than the Nyquist frequency. *Upsampling* increases the number of samples in a digital audio stream to approximate the effect of the signal having been sampled at a higher rate originally (Fig. 4.1).

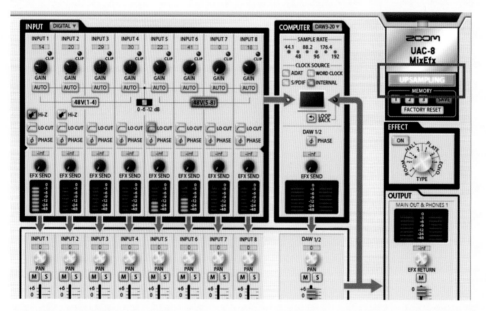

Figure 4.1   Zoom's UAC-8 performs four-times upsampling during both analog-to-digital and digital-to-analog conversion. For example, if the sampling frequency is 44.1 kHz, the UAC-8 processes the signal at 176.4 kHz.

With virtual instruments, it seems both are happening—what some companies refer to as "oversampling" is a process that involves upsampling the audio at a higher sample rate, rendering or processing it at a rate that's higher than the Nyquist frequency, then downsampling it back to the project's native sample rate.

So we'll use the term "oversampling" because it seems like a more comprehensive "umbrella" term for what's going on with virtual instruments. But don't let the wording distract you. The end result is that the plug-in sounds as if it were recorded at a higher sample rate.

Many modern virtual instruments and amp sims oversample, or have an option to do so (Fig. 4.2), so you'd think that would be the end of it—and most of the time, it is. However, there can be limitations with oversampling, especially for virtual instruments.

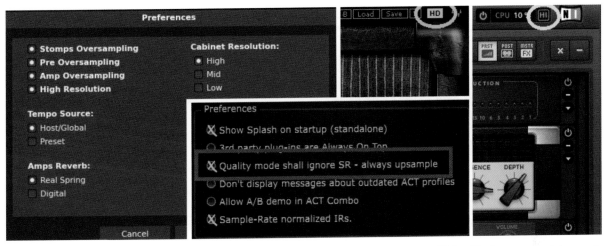

Figure 4.2 Four guitar amp simulators, clockwise from left: IK Multimedia AmpliTube Preferences set to apply oversampling to the stompbox effects, preamps, and/or amps for maximum resolution; Waves GTR high-definition button (circled in green); Native Instruments Guitar Rig's high-definition button (circled in blue), AMR ReValver Preferences set so that it always upsamples.

Although some instruments may perform 2x oversampling, that still might not be sufficient to eliminate foldover distortion on harmonically rich sources like pulse waves—so oversampling an oversampled instrument could still improve the sound. Furthermore, the sound quality of plug-ins that oversample depends on the quality of the sample-rate conversion algorithms. They have to work in real time, whereas offline sample-rate conversion algorithms can take as long as they want to do complex calculations.

 Oversampling draws more CPU power. Fortunately, oversampling is an optional preference in many plug-ins. If your CPU is struggling (or you have to choose a high latency setting), you can turn off oversampling while recording, and then turn it on during mixing when latency isn't as much of an issue.

Pros and Cons of Recording at Higher Sample Rates

Although it might seem the simplest solution is starting and completing projects at 96 kHz, there are pros and cons of recording at sample rates higher than 44.1 or 48 kHz.

Pros of Higher Sample Rates

♦ Under some circumstances, this may improve fidelity.

♦ Some people consider recording at a higher sample rate more "professional," although that may be more about perception than reality.

♦ Higher sample rates can reduce latency (a delay when monitoring through the computer) if the computer can handle higher sample rates as easily as lower ones.

Cons of Higher Sample Rates

♦ 96 kHz audio takes up over twice as much memory for storage as 44.1 kHz audio, all other aspects being equal.

♦ Running at 96 kHz stresses out the computer more, which reduces the potential track count.

♦ Some older plug-ins might not work at 88.2 kHz and above.

♦ A higher sample rate may not make any audible difference anyway.

I usually record at 44.1 kHz with 24-bit resolution. The computer runs smoothly, and projects don't need as much memory for storage (however, if clients want to work at 96 kHz, I accommodate them). Besides, for virtual instruments and amp sims, Appendix A describes a workaround to obtain the benefits of recording virtual instruments and amp sims at high sample rates in low-sample-rate projects.

Note that oversampling can't improve audio that already includes aliasing distortion (e.g., a sample with aliasing in a sample-playback instrument), because it's not an artifact produced within the computer—it's baked into the sound. The oversampling techniques we've covered apply only to audio that's "born" in the computer.

Similarly, it's unlikely that oversampling sounds recorded via a computer's audio interface will sound any better, because the audio interface itself will almost certainly filter out harmonics that could interfere with the sampling frequency. However, if someone believes recording a virtual instrument or signal processor at 96 kHz sounds better than recording it at 44.1 kHz, that may indeed be true—and yes, the difference can be obvious.

But also consider that you may not *want* the difference caused by recording an instrument or amp sim at a higher sample rate. When I did an oversampling demo at a seminar with a particular synthesizer, most people preferred the sound with the aliasing, because the oversampled sound was brighter than what they expected. Conversely, when oversampling an amp sim and also a different synth, the consensus was that the oversampled versions sounded much better.

Although oversampling isn't a panacea, it can improve the sound quality in certain circumstances. With many synths, oversampling makes no audible difference—but with others, you'll hear more clarity and sometimes a very different sound. As always, use your ears. After all, distortion isn't necessarily that horrible—think of how many guitar players wouldn't have a career without it.

Direct Stream Digital (DSD)

Multitrack recording software uses *PCM* (Pulse-Code Modulation) digital audio technology, which is what we've covered so far: sampling digital audio at a particular rate, and with a particular bit resolution. DSD is a different digital audio technology that uses a much higher clocking rate than PCM audio, with 1-bit audio pulses to encode analog levels into digital data.

The conversion process converts a waveform into a series of pulses with varying pulse widths (Fig. 4.3)

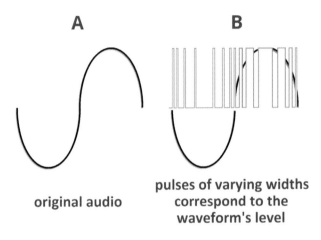

A **B**

pulses of varying widths
correspond to the
waveform's level

original audio

Figure 4.3 With DSD, a pulse indicates whether the level is going up or down. This image is simplified to get the concept across, but with DSD, the pulse rate is extremely high (at least 2,822,400 kHz). If drawn to scale, the pulses would be so close together that the image would look like a band of solid color.

Many audiophiles feel DSD sounds more "open," although maybe that's partly because the output smoothing filter doesn't have to be as steep as with PCM, thus reducing the possibility of coloration.

However, for multitrack home recording, DSD is pretty much a non-starter, because it's difficult (if not impossible) to do mixing, EQ, panning, and other common DSP-based operations. Most audio is recorded as PCM anyway, and then converted to DSD to capture the mix in the DSD format (Fig. 4.4).

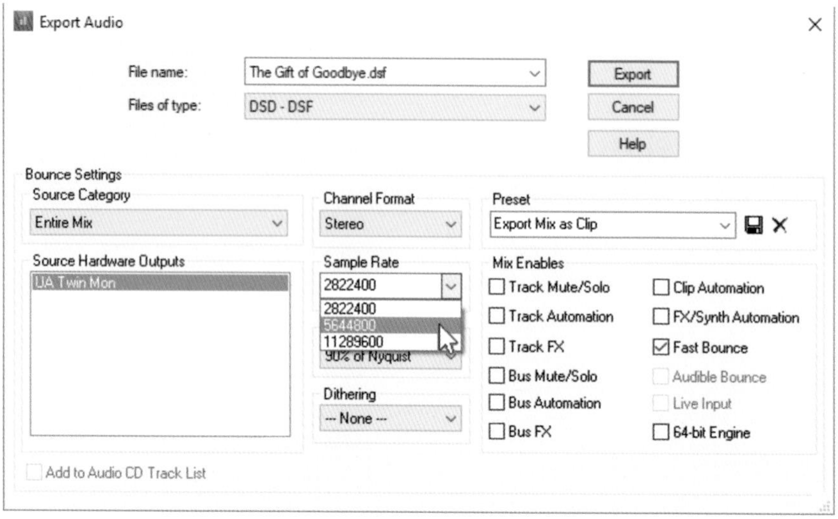

Figure 4.4 Cakewalk by BandLab is one of the few programs that can import and export DSD format files using the standard DSD rates of 2.8, 5.6, and 11.2 megahertz. However, all editing operations are done using standard PCM technology.

The Super Audio CD (SACD) is a commercial implementation of DSD technology, but it never enjoyed significant sales. There is a niche market (especially in Japan), and some companies continue to release SACD titles, but despite various attempts to revive it over the years, SACD will almost certainly never duplicate the CD's popularity.

___

Tech Talk: The Digital Downside—Fossil Formats

The rapid evolution of digital technology has left many digital audio formats obsolete. For example, Sony's recordable MiniDisc had a brief period of popularity until recordable CDs became common. The Digital Compact Cassette, intended as a replacement for the analog cassette, was a commercial failure. Tape-based digital multitrack recorders ruled the earth for about ten years, until computer-based, hard-disk recording became cost-effective.

Furthermore, some technologies (like surround audio) failed to connect with consumers. A PCM-based surround format, DVD-A, was touted along with SACD and Blu-Ray audio as ideal for surround. But DVD-A is extinct, and while Blu-Ray movies are popular, Blu-Ray audio is not. What's more, now that so many people listen to music over headphones, 5.1 surround will have an even harder time being accepted as an audio-only medium. The difficulty in setting up a quality 5.1 surround system in the home can also be a challenge. However, like SACD, audio surround releases have found a niche market.

___

Key Takeaways

♦ Although there are many sample rates, the most common ones are 44.1 kHz for CDs, and 96 kHz for "high-resolution" audio. 48 kHz is a common audio sample rate for video projects.

♦ Currently, sample rates above 96 kHz (e.g., 176.4, 192, and 384 kHz) are used mostly for stereo or surround live recordings of acoustic instruments and ensembles.

♦ The Nyquist Theorem states that a digital audio system can represent audio frequencies lower than half the sampling rate accurately. In other words, a 44.1 kHz system can accurately reproduce frequencies lower than 22.050 kHz.

♦ Foldover distortion can occur when audio is at a frequency that interferes with a project's sample rate.

♦ With plug-ins that generate sound "in the box," there are some circumstances where recording at a higher sample rate makes an audible improvement because it eliminates the possibility of foldover distortion. This doesn't seem to occur with sounds recorded through an audio interface, which limits bandwidth anyway.

♦ Some hardware oversamples (multiplies the existing sample rate) to give the benefits of recording at a higher sample rate. Virtual instruments can also oversample to increase fidelity.

♦ Higher sample rates are not without drawbacks, because their files require more space for storage, and stress computers more.

♦ Direct Stream Digital is another type of digital audio technology, but it never found a mass market.

Chapter 5

Bit Resolution

Another aspect of the conversion process, *bit resolution* (also called *bit depth* or less commonly, *word length*), specifies the accuracy with which an analog-to-digital converter measures an input signal. A good analogy is a ruler's calibrations. A ruler calibrated in inches can measure only whole inches with accuracy, but a ruler calibrated in sixteenths of an inch can measure with 16 times better resolution.

With digital audio, each sample measures a signal's instantaneous voltage. The more precise the measurement, the more accurate the conversion from analog audio into digital data.

Resolution varies among audio systems. Higher resolution requires more memory to store larger numbers, as well as greater analog-to-digital converter accuracy to take advantage of the higher resolution. Because memory and converters have become less expensive, gear in general has gravitated toward higher bit resolutions.

For comparison purposes, an audio greeting card may have audio with only four bits of resolution. Early digital audio systems used eight bits. 12-bit samplers were common, and 12 bits was considered the minimum acceptable resolution for working with digital audio. CDs use 16-bit resolution, and high-resolution audio uses 24-bit resolution.

 Although a 24-bit file requires 50% more storage than a 16-bit file (at the same sample rate), most recording engineers agree that 24-bit recording is preferable to 16-bit recording.

Tech Talk: About Binary Math

Bits are the basic units of binary math. It's not necessary to know how binary math works to record music, but the following may help demystify this aspect of digital audio.

Our standard decimal number system has ten digits: 0, 1, 2, 3, 4, 5, 6, 7, 8, and 9. With numbers that include more than one decimal place, a digit's position is important. The right-most position is units, the next position to the left is tens, the next position to the left is hundreds, and so on.

For example, the number 368 expresses a large number using only three digits, because each digit has a multiplier—368 is really expressing $(3 \times 100) + (6 \times 10) + (8 \times 1) = 368$.

Binary math uses only two values for each digit: 0 and 1. Each column in a multi-digit binary number is a bit, and represents two times the column to the right. The right-most column can represent one of two values: 0 or 1. Adding a "twos" column to the left gives twice as many potential values:

00 binary = 0 decimal

01 binary = 1 decimal

10 binary = 2 decimal

11 binary = 3 decimal

Each column added to the left doubles the number of possible values (each column represents another bit). As shown above, including two columns (for a two-bit number) allows us to represent four possible values. Increasing to three bits allows us to represent twice as many possibilities, up to eight values. Using four bits lets us represent 16 values, five bits can represent 32 values, and so on. The more bits, the greater the potential resolution—being able to resolve an analog signal to sixteen values gives more accuracy than two values. Of course, we need more than sixteen values to measure analog audio accurately.

Here's a list showing bit depth versus resolution for common audio bit depths. From the following, it's clear that at least theoretically, a 24-bit number can measure levels with 256 times greater precision than a 16-bit number.

4 bits = 16 values	14 bits = 16,384 values	20 bits = 1,048,576 values
8 bits = 256 values	16 bits = 65,536 values	22 bits = 4,194,304 values
12 bits = 4,096 values	18 bits = 262,144 values	24 bits = 16,777,216 values

Distortion and Bit Resolution

The lower the bit resolution, the greater the potential distortion—if you can't measure a signal accurately, then you can't reproduce it accurately. This leads to distortion.

However, unlike distortion in the physical world (which tends to increase with higher signal levels), digital distortion increases with *lower* signal levels, because there are fewer bits available for measuring the voltage (Fig. 5.1).

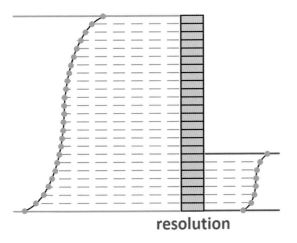

resolution

Figure 5.1 For a fixed amount of resolution, as happens with hardware like A/D and D/A converters, you can define a high-amplitude signal (left) with more precision than a low-amplitude signal (right).

Fortunately, the lower the signal level, the harder it is to hear and differentiate between a distorted and undistorted sound. Also, a technique called *dithering* (described later in this chapter) can reduce the perceived amount of distortion on playback. Most importantly, the audio engine inside your program isn't bound by the rules of hardware, and can offer essentially unlimited resolution when processing signals internally within your computer. We'll cover this in more detail shortly.

Accuracy vs. Resolution

Although some consider these two terms as equivalent, they are not necessarily the same. 24-bit resolution theoretically has about 144 dB of dynamic range (approximately 6 dB per bit), and in theory, its 16,777,216 values are all equally spaced. But in the real world, that's not true, because 24 bits reaches the technical limits of analog-to-digital and digital-to-analog converters. No 24-bit converter truly delivers 24 bits of resolution; noise can reduce the dynamic range, circuit board layout can result in interference for low-level signals, and manufacturing tolerances for analog-to-digital and digital-to-analog converters may mean that the 16,777,216 divisions are not all equally spaced. These errors are small (some would say insignificant), and accuracy has improved dramatically over the years, but be aware that digital circuity isn't perfect (yet).

Tech Talk: Dynamic Range and Bit Depth

It's often said that each bit of resolution represents 6 dB of dynamic range. However, an ideal ADC with no input signal would produce an output of all zeroes, thereby resulting in an infinitely wide dynamic range (dividing the maximum output by zero yields an infinitely high number).

For digital converters, the *true* dynamic range is defined as (brace yourself!) ten times the log of the ratio of full-scale signal power to quantization-noise power (i.e., the dominant noise when a signal is present). We won't go through the math (you can thank me later), but suffice it to say, this works out to:

Dynamic range = (6.02 × N) + 1.76

...where N is the number of bits. Based on this equation, an ideal 16-bit system has a dynamic range of 98.08 dB. As a rule of thumb, 6 dB per bit is a close approximation... and that's good enough for me.

As a result, a 24-bit converter will more likely deliver a real-world resolution between 20 and 22 bits, which is more than sufficient for high-quality audio. You'll also see references to 32-bit and 64-bit resolution, but that usually refers to the resolution inside a digital system (see next section), not the resolution involved in exchanging data between the analog and digital worlds.

Hardware Resolution vs. Recording Software Resolution

This is a common source of confusion. The resolution of a hardware signal processor or audio interface specifies the accuracy with which it can capture and play back audio. The *recording software resolution,* also called *audio engine resolution, process resolution,* or *processing resolution,* is different from, and can be independent of, the resolution of the hardware that connects to your digital system. The audio engine resolution is usually much higher—typically 32-bit, 64-bit, and sometimes more—because the software has to handle complex mathematical operations.

A function like changing level involves multiplying and dividing the numbers that represent digital audio. So, it's easy to end up with totals that require higher resolution. By way of example, consider the following calculations: if you multiply 2 × 2, you need only 1 digit to represent the result (4). But if you multiply 2 × 9—both single-digit numbers—you will need *two* digits to represent the result of 18.

Even though most hardware audio processors and interfaces offer 24-bit resolution, it's generally best to set your recording program's resolution as high as the software allows so that any calculations are as accurate as possible. The most common choices are *32-bit floating point, 64-bit,* and *64-bit floating point.* For all *practical* purposes, the results obtained with any of these three options are more or less equivalent.

Although some people will insist that you have to use the highest possible resolution, and while it may make a difference in some "corner cases," 32-bit floating-point or higher will be fine.

Tech Talk: Floating-Point Arithmetic

This is a way to process digital data with greater speed and accuracy. *Floating-point arithmetic* can express very large or very small numbers with fewer digits, which relieves stress on a computer's computational abilities. This may speed up processing as well as provide better resolution. It's not necessary to get into the weeds with this, but you can think of it as conceptually similar to scientific notation, which allows expressing extremely large or small numbers with fewer digits.

Headroom in Digital Systems

The audio engine inside your program has an almost unlimited dynamic range. However, audio going into or coming out of your computer also goes through hardware—and even modern audio hardware doesn't have an infinite dynamic range. To prevent exceeding the dynamic range, it's good practice to allow for some *headroom*—the difference in level between a signal's peak and the maximum level that a preamp, analog-to-digital converter, or digital-to-analog converter can handle.

For example, if a signal's peaks reach 0 on your software's virtual meters when recording, then it has used up the interface's available headroom prior to entering your computer. Any additional level increases at the interface will result in distortion. (Digital distortion is particularly nasty, because it sounds harsher than the type of distortion associated with tube amps and most analog circuitry.) On the other hand, if the peaks register as –6 dB, then there's 6 dB of headroom prior to the onset of distortion.

 When recording, many engineers recommend setting digital audio levels at least 6 dB below 0 (or lower—peak levels of –12 dB or –15 dB are common).

During playback, keep a digital mixer's master fader close to 0, and adjust levels within individual channels to prevent overloads when the master output feeds your audio interface for playback. This is a better way of managing levels than keeping the channel faders high and then reducing the master gain to bring the output level down to 0 dB (or preferably, somewhat lower).

When mixing, another good reason to leave a few dB of headroom at the master output, and not run levels right up to 0 dB, is that most digital metering measures the level of the digital audio samples, which may not reflect the actual analog output. Converting digital audio back to analog may result in higher values than the samples themselves, which creates *intersample distortion.* Unless your channel's meters can alert you to intersample distortion, it is a good practice to leave a few dB of headroom to avoid this.

Tech Talk: Intersample Distortion

This type of distortion can occur with samples that use up the maximum available headroom, when these samples then pass through the digital-to-analog converter's output-smoothing filter to reconstruct the original waveform. The reconstructed waveform might have a higher amplitude than the peak level of the samples, which means the waveform now exceeds the maximum available headroom (Fig. 5.2).

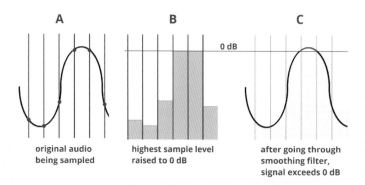

Figure 5.2 With the analog audio waveform sampled in (A), raising the digital audio's level to the maximum available headroom (B) can exceed the maximum headroom when going through the smoothing filter (C) that reconstructs the analog waveform.

DC Offset

DC offset isn't a particularly sexy topic, nor is it a particularly common problem. But it can be the culprit behind issues related to reduced headroom such as mastering oddities, pops and clicks, effects that don't process properly, and other gremlins.

Background: DC Offset in the Analog Era

We'll jump into the DC offset story during the 70s, when *op amps*—analog integrated circuits that packed a tremendous amount of gain in a small, inexpensive package with (typically) two inputs and one output—became popular. Theoretically, with no input signal, the inputs and output are at exactly zero volts. But due to imperfections within the op amp itself, or DC present at the output of the stage feeding the op amp, sometimes there can be several millivolts of DC present at one of the inputs.

Normally this wouldn't matter, but if the op amp is providing lots of gain, even a tiny voltage at the input could end up as a significant output voltage. For example, with +0.002 volts of offset at the input, an op amp providing 60 dB of gain (an amplification factor of 1,000) will have +2 volts of offset at the output. If the op amp had ±10 volts of headroom with no input signal, the +2V of offset reduces the positive headroom to only +8 volts. So the signal can't exceed ±8 volts, instead of ±10 volts. We've lost 20% of the available headroom.

DC Offset in Digital Systems

With digital audio, there are two main ways DC offset can infiltrate a signal.

♦ Recording an analog signal with DC offset into an interface whose low-frequency response goes all the way down to DC (rather than rolling off below a low frequency, like 20 Hz).

♦ Inaccuracies in the ADC or conversion subsystem that add DC offset to a file brought into the computer. As with analog circuits, a plug-in that provides lots of gain (like amp sim distortion) can turn a small amount of offset into something major.

In either case, offset appears as a signal baseline that doesn't match up with the true 0-volt baseline (Fig. 5.3).

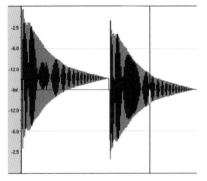

Figure 5.3 With these two drum hits, the first one has a significant amount of DC offset. The second has been corrected to remove DC offset. Because more headroom is available, the second hit can now reach a higher peak level than the first drum hit, whose positive peak uses up the maximum available headroom.

Digital technology has also created a new type of offset issue that's technically more of a subsonic problem than "genuine" DC offset, but nonetheless causes similarly negative effects. As one example, I once transposed a sliding oscillator tone so far down, it added what looked like a slowly varying DC offset to the signal, which limited the headroom (Fig. 5.4).

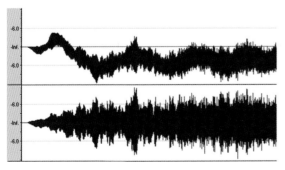

Figure 5.4 The top signal is the original *normalized* version (i.e., its peaks use up the available headroom), while the lower one has that version processed by a steep low-cut filter at 20 Hz, and then re-normalized. Note that the lower waveform's overall level is much greater.

In addition to reduced headroom, two other major problems are associated with DC offset in digitally-based systems:

♦ When transitioning between two pieces of digital audio, one with a DC offset and one without (or with a different amount of offset), there will likely be a pop or click at the transition point.

♦ Effects or processes requiring a signal that's symmetrical around zero will not work as effectively. For example, a distortion plug-in that clips positive and negative peaks will clip them unevenly if there's a DC offset. Also, a noise gate or "strip silence" function will need a higher (or lower) threshold than normal in order to exceed not just the noise, but the noise plus the offset value.

Digital Solutions

There are three main ways to solve DC offset problems with software-based digital audio programs:

♦ Most pro-level digital audio editing and multitrack recording software includes a DC offset correction function, generally found under a "processing" menu, along with functions like change gain, reverse, flip phase, etc. (Fig. 5.5). This may also be made available as a plug-in. The processor analyzes the signal and adds or subtracts the required correction to make sure that 0 really is 0.

Figure 5.5 Like most programs, Cakewalk by BandLab's audio processing includes the option to remove DC offset from audio clips. Here, the DC offset was down by –85.3 dB in one channel and –81.6 in the other. After removing DC offset, the readings were around –103 dB.

♦ Apply a steep high-pass filter that cuts off everything below 20 Hz or so. (Even with a comparatively gentle 12 dB/octave filter, a signal at 0.5 Hz will be down more than 60 dB.) In practice, it's not a bad idea to cut the subsonic part of the spectrum anyway. Most speakers can't reproduce signals this low, so they just use up bandwidth.

♦ Select a 2 to 10 millisecond region at the beginning and end of the file or segment with the offset, and then apply a fade-in and fade-out. This will create an envelope that starts and ends at 0, respectively. It won't get rid of the DC offset component within the file (so you still have the restricted headroom problem), but at least you won't hear a pop at transitions.

DC offset usually isn't a major problem. But every now and then, DC offset will rear its ugly head in a way that you *do* notice. And now you know what to do about it.

File Bit Resolution

When working with digital audio, you'll often want to import or export digital audio files. Your recording or editing software may allow choosing specific resolutions for the files you record, import, or export. For example, with a live recording of a rock band, 16-bit audio may be sufficient (after all, the noise floor of a live recording will almost certainly result in a dynamic range that fits easily within a CD's 16-bit resolution). Recording with 16-bit file resolution creates projects that take up less space than recording at higher resolutions. If you're using a 24-bit audio interface, the software will just ignore the eight least significant bits. On the other hand, to record a source like an acoustic jazz trio with the maximum available headroom, you'd select 24 bits for the software's file resolution to match the audio interface's maximum resolution. (Remember, this doesn't affect the resolution of the software's audio engine, as applied to mixing and other operations—only the resolution of files entering into your project.)

Similarly, you can often choose the *render* or *export* bit depth. This is the bit resolution of, for example, a bounced or exported file. CDs require 16-bit audio, so even if you recorded a project with 24-bit resolution, you would render your mixes with 16-bit resolution if they're intended for CD. The rendering process would discard the eight least significant bits, and probably apply dithering (discussed next) to simulate a greater bit depth.

Rendering at a greater bit depth does not increase a file's resolution. If you record a 16-bit file and export it as a 24-bit file, unless there's processing applied during the rendering, you'll end up with a 24-bit file whose last eight bits will all have a value of 0.

Tech Talk: Confirmation Bias

A lot of discussion around digital audio falls into the "how many angels can dance on the head of a pin" category. Some people will insist that recording with 32- or 64-bit files sounds better; that may be the case. However, the mind is a powerful force, and there's a phenomenon known as *confirmation bias*—the tendency to interpret results as confirming a particular belief. For example, if someone wants to believe 64-bit audio resolution sounds better than 32-bit resolution, they'll convince themselves the 64-bit file sounds better and also *believe* that it does. The only way to know for sure whether one option is better than another is to conduct double–blind, scientifically controlled testing. Much of the time all these prove is that some "improvements" are in the ear of the beholder.

As an example of the power of the human mind, once while I was mixing a song, the lead guitarist insisted the solo needed to be louder. I felt it was already too loud, but "the customer is always right." So, while he was out of the room, I moved the "Lead Gtr" label on the mixer channel to a different channel that had no audio input, and set the fader to the same level as the real lead guitar channel.

When the guitarist came back in, I said, "You know, I think you're right, let's increase the volume a bit." I then moved the fader up very slowly on the bogus channel, which of course wasn't changing the level at all. But once it reached a certain point, the guitarist said, "Yes! Leave it there. That's the right level. See, I *told* you it needed more level!" Not only did I humbly agree, I was even able to keep a straight face.

Another example is a famous experiment involving wine tasting, led by Hilke Plassmann from the California Institute of Technology. When the same wine was put in bottles clearly marked with their prices, experienced wine tasters said the "expensive" wine tasted better, and they derived more pleasure from it.

Regarding audio, try not to be influenced into thinking that when a plug-in has beautiful 3D graphics, it sounds better. Granted, looking better can be more inspirational—and that's a valid consideration. But don't always trust your eyes. Just ask that lead guitarist... or those wine tasters!

Dithering Demystified

Early digital audio devices, like the CD, had 16-bit resolution and a 44.1 kHz sampling rate. Similarly, digital recording systems of that era often did their internal processing at 16/44.1, which was a problem—every operation (such as changing levels or applying EQ) rounded off the result to 16 bits. If you did enough operations, these roundoff errors could accumulate and add a "fuzziness" to the sound.

The next step forward was increasing the internal resolution of digital audio systems. If a mathematical operation created an *overflow* result that required more than 16 bits, no problem: 24-, 32-, 64-, and even 128-bit internal processing became commonplace (Fig. 5.6). As long as the audio stayed within the system, running out of resolution wasn't an issue.

Figure 5.6 With PreSonus Studio One's audio mixing and processing engine, you can select 32-bit, single-precision, floating-point resolution, or 64-bit, double-precision, floating-point resolution.

Today's hard disk recorders most likely record and play back with at least 32-bit floating-point resolution. The rest of your gear (digital mixer, digital synth, etc.) probably has fairly high internal resolution as well. But currently, although there are some high-resolution audio formats intended for consumers, your mix usually ends up streaming online in MP3 or AAC format, or in the world's most common physical delivery medium (at least for now)—a 16-bit, 44.1 kHz CD.

Before the advent of dithering, an audio file's "extra" bits were simply truncated and discarded. This meant that, for example, decay tails below the 16-bit limit just stopped abruptly. Maybe you've heard a buzzing sort of sound at the end of a fade-out or reverb tail; that's the sound of the signal running out of resolution.

One reason you hear this buzzing with truncated signals is that the least significant bit, which tries to follow the audio signal, switches back and forth between 0 and 1. This buzzing is called *quantization noise*, because the noise occurs while quantizing the audio into discrete steps. In a 24-bit recording, the lower 8 bits beyond 16 bits account for additional possible levels between the "on" and "off" condition; but once the recording has been truncated, the resolution is no longer there to reproduce those additional levels.

However, note that these are very low-level signals. For that punk rock-industrial-dance mix where all the meters are in the red, you probably don't need even 16 bits of resolution. But when you're trying to record the ambient reverb tail of an acoustic space, low-level resolution can matter.

Dithering to the Rescue

Dithering is a process that adds a controlled type of noise to the lowest-level signals, thus using the data in those least significant bits to influence the sound of the more significant bits. It's almost as if, even though the least significant bits are gone, their spirit lives on in the recording's sound.

Cutting off the least significant bits is called *truncation*, and some proponents of dithering believe that dithering somehow sidesteps the truncation process. That's a misconception. Dithered or not, when a 24-bit signal ends up on a 16-bit CD, eight bits are truncated and never heard from again. Nonetheless, there's a difference between flat-out truncation, and truncation with dithering.

How to Hear the Results of Dithering

Dithering happens at a really low level, so you need to generate low-level audio to hear what digital audio sounds like with extremely low resolution, as well as what it sounds like when you add dithering.

Here's how to generate a suitable test file and evaluate the effect of dithering:

1.   Load an audio file that uses up most of your recording software or digital audio editor's available headroom (i.e., the file is normalized so the peak values are close to 0).

2.   Reduce the file's level by –80 dB. Your software may not allow reducing the level by this much, so you may need to (for example) reduce the level by –40 dB, and then reduce it again by another –40 dB.

3. Export this as a 16-bit, 44.1 kHz file to generate a low-level audio file suitable for testing.

4. Import this file into your DAW or digital audio editor, which should be set for at least 24-bit internal resolution.

5. Normalize the test file to 0, and it should sound horrible—buzzy and distorted.

6. Undo the normalization so the file is back to its super-low level.

7. Export the file as several test files with different types of dither. Load these test files, normalize them up to 0 dB, and you'll hear how dithering affects the sound. Of course, there will now be noise... but the end result should sound better than the nasty, buzzing distortion of undithered audio (Fig. 5.7).

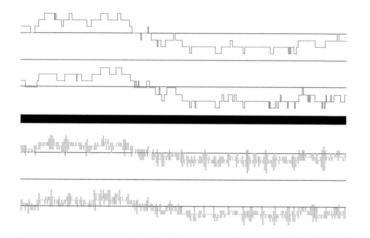

Figure 5.7 Both waveforms above were set to a peak of –80 dB, exported, then imported and amplified so their peaks hit 0 dB. The upper waveform has no dithering, and sounds spiky and distorted. The lower waveform has dithering applied. Note how the waveform looks smoother—it sounds smoother, too.

Tech Talk: How Dithering Works

Let's assume you have a 24-bit recorded signal. Dithering adds random noise to the 24-bit signal's lowest eight bits. This noise is different for the two channels, to avoid degrading the stereo separation.

It may seem odd that adding noise can improve the sound, but one analogy is the bias signal used in analog tape. Analog tape is linear (mostly distortionless) over a narrow range. Distortion occurs if you hit the tape too hard with high-level audio, but signals *below* a certain minimum level can also sound distorted. The bias signal adds a constant supersonic signal (so we don't hear it) whose level sits at the lower threshold of the tape's linear region. Any low-level signals add to the bias signal, which boosts them into the linear region, where they can be heard without distortion.

Adding noise to the lower eight bits increases their amplitude and pushes some of the information contained in those bits into the higher bits. Therefore, the lowest part of the dynamic range no longer correlates directly to the original signal, but to a combination of the noise source and information present in the lowest eight bits. This reduces the quantization noise, providing in its place a smoother type of hiss modulated by the lower-level information. The most obvious audible benefit is that fades become smoother and more realistic, but there's also more sonic detail.

Although adding noise may seem like a bad idea, psycho-acoustic principles are on our side. Because any noise added by the dithering process has a constant level and frequency content, our ears have an easy time picking out the content (signal) from the noise. We've lived with noise long enough that a little bit hanging around at −90 dB or so is tolerable, particularly if it allows us to hear a subjectively extended dynamic range.

Noise Shaping and Different Dithering Types

There are different types of dithering noise, which have varying degrees of audibility. The dither may be wideband, thus trading off the lowest possible distortion for slightly higher perceived noise. A narrower band of noise will sound quieter, but will allow some low-level distortion to remain.

To make dithering even less noticeable, *noise shaping* distributes noise across the audio spectrum so that the bulk of it lies where the ear is least sensitive (i.e., the higher frequencies). Some noise shaping curves are extremely complex—they're not just a straight line, but dip down in regions of maximum hearing sensitivity (typically the midrange).

Mastering programs like IK Multimedia's T-RackS (Fig. 5.8) and many DAWs offer multiple "flavors" of dithering.

Figure 5.8 This mastering processor offers four types of dither. The master file is 24 bit. Because it's being converted to a lower bit resolution (16 bits), the dithering options become available.

Again, this recalls the analogy of analog tape's bias signal, which is usually around 100 kHz to keep it out of the audible range. We can't use those kinds of frequencies in a system that samples at 44.1 kHz or even 96 kHz, but several noise-shaping algorithms push the signal as high as possible, short of hitting the Nyquist frequency (i.e., half the sample rate, which is the highest frequency that can be recorded and played back at a given sample rate).

Different manufacturers use different noise-shaping algorithms; often the differences are extremely subtle. Sometimes you'll have a choice of dithering *and* noise-shaping algorithms, so you can choose the combination that works best for specific types of program material. Not all of these algorithms are created equal, nor do they sound equal. But again, remember, we're dealing with very low levels. Many people hear no difference between truncated and dithered audio.

How to Apply Dithering

You need dithering *only* when converting a high bit-resolution source format to one with lower resolution, and you apply it only once. Typically, this is from your high-resolution master or mix to a 16-bit, mixed-for-CD format.

If you're given an already dithered 16-bit file to edit, and you edit it in a program with 24-bit resolution, that 16-bit file already contains dithered data, and the higher-resolution editor should preserve it. When it's time to convert the edited version back down to 16 bits, render the existing file without dithering.

Another consideration is if you give a mastering or duplication facility two dithered 16-bit files to be crossfaded. Crossfading the dithered sections could lead to artifacts; it's better to crossfade the two files prior to dithering, and then dither the combination.

Check any programs you use to see if dithering is enabled by default, or if it is enabled and saved as a preference. In general, you want to leave dithering off and enable it only when needed.

Be careful to check whether two plug-ins are dithering at the same time. You want dithering to be the signal chain's last processor, and preferably, to be post-master fader. Steinberg Wavelab includes an Apogee-designed UV22 plug-in that's intended to insert after the final level control.

However, suppose you insert another plug-in prior to the UV22, like the Waves L3 Ultramaximizer (which not only includes dithering, but has dithering enabled by default). Unless you disable the dithering in the L3 Ultramaximizer plug-in (Fig. 5.9), you'll be "doubling up" on dithering. (Another option to prevent this would be to use the L3's dithering, rather than the UV22 plug-in.)

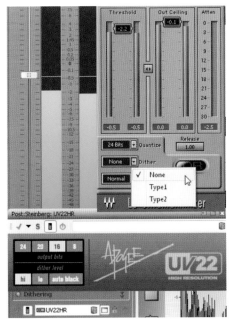

Figure 5.9 If you use Wavelab's internal dithering, don't enable dithering in any other master effects plug-ins. (In this screenshot, the dithering in Waves' L3 Ultramaximizer has been turned off.)

If your music includes wide, natural dynamics, proper dithering can indeed give a sweeter, smoother sound, free of digital quantization distortion when you downsize to 16 bits.

Data Compression and Audio

Audio files take up a fair amount of storage space. When Apple's iPod portable music player appeared in 2001, memory was far more expensive than it is now, and the first iPods had only 5 GB of memory—enough to hold eight typical CDs. Concurrently, the dot-com boom was taking off, and people wanted to send audio files over the internet. But bandwidth and speed were limited, so sending full-resolution files was time-consuming.

The MP3 Audio Format

In the mid-1990s, the MP3 audio encoding format had evolved into a standardized method to reduce audio file size. This encoding technology uses sophisticated data compression algorithms to reduce the amount of data needed to reproduce music. (Note that this has nothing to do with audio *dynamic range* compression, as used in mixing to alter an audio file's dynamic range.)

Data compression is a bit of a misnomer, because this technology uses data *omission* algorithms. They don't work like the ZIP or RAR data compression algorithms, which restore the original file when uncompressed. Instead, a process like MP3 throws away "unneeded" data, which is why it's called a *lossy* process. For example, if there's a lot of high-level sound going on, the algorithm might assume you can't hear lower-level material, and decide that for those sections, you need only 24 dB of dynamic range. This requires only four bits of resolution—25% the amount of data required by 16-bit resolution.

Data-compressed music compromises fidelity; however, you can usually choose the amount of compression to be applied. Light compression can reduce the file size, yet still sound like uncompressed audio to the average person. Heavy compression can really shrink file sizes, but you'll likely hear artifacts not present in the uncompressed music. When the iPod appeared, compression that reduced file sizes by 90% was common. This is why the original iPod could truthfully claim "1,000 songs in your pocket" with only 5 GB of memory.

There are also lossless data compression algorithms, such as FLAC (Free Lossless Audio Codec) and the lossless audio format options offered by Microsoft and Apple, that don't throw away any data. When uncompressed, these revert to the original file. However, these formats don't provide as much data reduction; with complex music, the size reduction may be only 10 to 20%.

Data Compression Formats

Although there are many data compression algorithms for audio, only a few are common:

- ♦ **MP3.** This allows several levels of encoding, so you can generate just about any size audio file—with lower fidelity as the files get smaller. There are many free or shareware MP3 players (e.g., iTunes and Windows Groove Music); for MP3 encoding, you can use iTunes, most digital audio editors, and many digital audio workstations.

  For several decades, the algorithms behind MP3 had patent protection and required licensing. However, most patents have now expired—some programs that used to charge extra for MP3 encoding to cover license fees no longer do so.

  When creating audio content for posting, MP3 is a good choice—not only can you choose the level of quality, but virtually all media players can read it, there's a ton of supporting software, and people can load the files into portable MP3 players.

- ♦ **AAC.** As the iPod's native file format, AAC remains popular and prevalent. Many people feel it sounds better than MP3 for a given file size. iTunes can convert uncompressed files to AAC.

- ♦ **Windows Media Audio.** Being part of Windows helped establish WMA in its early years, but it's not as common as MP3 or AAC, and few musicians post their music as WMA format files. (However because it did get traction, most new cars still recognize WMA files on USB memory sticks that are compatible with the car's audio system.) At low bit rates, the quality is generally better than MP3, and some feel it sounds better than AAC as well.

  Although Microsoft no longer offers a WMA player for the Mac, the utility Flip4Mac (a free version is available) can play Windows Media formats on Macs.

◆ **Ogg Vorbis.** While rare, this format also sounds better than MP3 for a given bit rate—and unlike MP3, the encoding tools (from the Xiph.Org Foundation) have always been free to developers.

Ogg Vorbis files haven't received much public acceptance, but the format has been embraced by some tech-savvy users.

◆ **FLAC.** Starting with Windows 10, this popular lossless compression format became the audio file format of choice for Windows. Musicians often use FLAC to send files back and forth when collaborating. Apple has a lossless variation on AAC.

Choosing the Right Encoder Settings

Audio files require encoding to create compressed formats; various parameters define the encoding quality. When encoding a file to any compressed format, always give the encoder high-quality, uncompressed material to work with so it can make the best decisions on how to apply the compression algorithm. Then choose the compression parameter values carefully.

When saving to MP3, you can typically choose from a range of *bit rates.* These represent the number of bits that get transferred in a second, from 320 kbps stereo (excellent quality, but largest resulting file size) down to 8 kbps mono (good enough for dictation).

Compressing a standard 28 MB WAV audio file to 320 kbps stereo MP3 results in a 6.4 MB file; compressing to 8 kbps mono yields a 0.16 MB file—a data reduction ratio of 175:1 (Fig. 5.10).

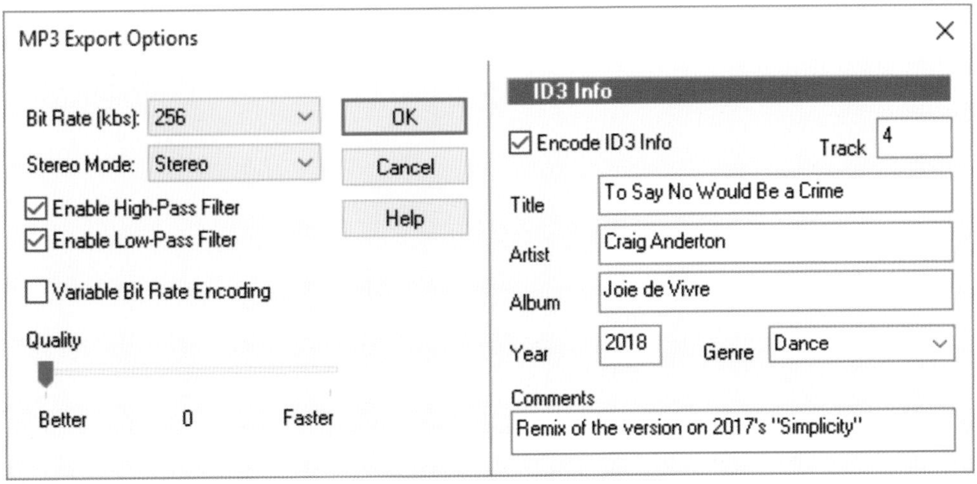

Figure 5.9 This public-domain MP3 encoder has been set to export a file at 256 kbps—a good tradeoff between file size and fidelity. "ID3 Info" includes the tags that show up in file players (e.g., portable music players) that display the album title, song, and artist.

128 kbps used to be the "internet standard" for stereo files posted online. However with online speed increasing and memory becoming less of a concern, there's been a tendency to use higher rates, like 192, 256, or even 320 kbps.

In addition to fixed rates, there are variable bit rate (VBR) options that optimize the bit stream dynamically, according to the material being played back. This is not as universally compatible, so it's preferable to use constant bit rates for anything where you want to reach the widest possible audience.

If your goal is a small file size, encode a file using a variety of bit rates and sampling frequencies, in mono and stereo, and audition the results to determine which parameter settings hit the sweet spot of best sound quality and smallest file size. Note that mono will usually have higher fidelity than stereo for a given file size. For example, with an MP3 128 kbps file, the mono version "spends" that bandwidth on a single, high-quality file. Stereo generates two 64 kbps streams—one for each channel—and 64 kbps doesn't sound as good as 128 kbps. However, getting the higher bit rate without increasing file size requires giving up stereo, which you may not want to do.

 Dithering a master file is appropriate for converting something like a 24-bit file to MP3, but it's important to use basic dithering options like triangular or rectangular. Noise-shaped dithering can interfere with the data compression process.

Converting to a Compressed Format with iTunes

Although there are plenty of ways to convert files to a compressed audio format like MP3, iTunes provides a free, cross-platform (Mac and Windows), and readily available option.

 If you don't already have iTunes installed, you can download it from www.apple.com, and then follow the instructions for installation.

Convert files with iTunes using the following procedure:

1. Open iTunes.

2. Drag the files you want to convert into the main iTunes window.

3. From the menu bar, choose *Edit > Preferences,* and then click on the *General* tab.

4. Click on the *Import Settings* button.

5. Choose the desired format with the *Import Using* pop-up menu. To illustrate how this works, we'll convert to MP3.

6. Choose the MP3 settings from the *Setting* pop-up menu. If you want to keep it simple, select one of the default data rate settings of 128kbps, 160kbps, or 192kbps. The higher the data rate, the better the fidelity (and bigger the file). Custom provides multiple options (Fig. 5.11).

Figure 5.10 iTunes' Import Settings dialog box is where you can choose the file format, and then choose its custom settings (the window in the lower right).

7. After choosing the Custom settings, you'll be presented with the following choices:

- **Stereo Bit Rate (data rate).** This is variable from 16kbps to 320kbps. The higher the rate, the higher the fidelity and the more space taken up by the file.

- **Use Variable Bit Rate Encoding.** This varies the number of bits used to store the file, based on the program material's needs. Although this kind of encoding can create smaller file sizes, VBR files are not compatible with all MP3 players, so it's probably best to leave this unchecked. If you do select this, another pop-up menu specifies the sound quality.

- **Sample Rate.** Selecting Auto chooses the same sample rate as the source material, which is usually the best choice. Choosing a lower sample rate than the source creates a smaller file size with the tradeoff being reduced fidelity; choosing a higher sample rate than the source creates a bigger file size, with no audible benefit.

- **Channels.** Auto creates a mono file from a mono source, and a stereo file from a stereo source, so this is usually the best option. For higher-quality audio with the same bit rate, you can choose mono, although you'll lose any stereo effects.

- **Stereo Mode.** This is available only if you choose Stereo for channels. At bit rates under 160 kbps, the Joint Stereo option can improve sound quality by not devoting unneeded bandwidth to redundant material.

- **Smart Encoding Adjustments.** This causes iTunes to analyze the encoding settings and source material, and then make what it feels are appropriate adjustments. Uncheck this if you're doing custom settings.

- **Filter Frequencies Below 10 Hz.** I recommend leaving this on, because even if your source material does contain frequencies below 10 Hz, very few transducers can play back frequencies that low. Therefore, there's no need to waste bandwidth on encoding subsonic frequencies.

8. Once the encoding parameters are set up, encode your file. In the main iTunes window, select the file. Then, choose *File > Convert > Create [file format you chose] Version.*

There's no obvious indication of file format in iTunes. If in the future you aren't sure which is the original and which is the MP3 copy, right-click (ctrl-click) on the name and select *Song Info*. Click the *File* button, and you'll see the format, sample rate, bit rate, size, duration, and other info.

Key Takeaways

- Bit resolution specifies the measurement accuracy of a signal's levels.

- More bits give higher resolution, but high-resolution files require more storage space.

- The maximum *practical* bit resolution is limited by today's technology. For example, a 24-bit ADC doesn't give 24 bits of resolution, but probably somewhere between 20 and 22 bits.

- Most engineers use 24-bit resolution when recording audio.

- Audio interfaces typically have less resolution than the audio engines in recording software, because the latter have to do complex mathematical operations involving high resolution—which can produce results requiring even higher resolution.

- Like analog audio, digital audio is ultimately subject to headroom limitations. It's best to leave some headroom for a variety of reasons, one of them being to avoid intersample distortion.

- DC offset can reduce headroom and/or lead to clicks and pops. While usually not a major problem, pro-level digital audio programs have a way to reduce or remove DC offset.

- Most programs can import and export audio at resolutions other than their native resolutions. For example, even if you record a file with 24-bit resolution, you might want to export with 16-bit resolution to accommodate the CD format.

♦ Dithering adds controlled, very low-level noise to minimize distortion that occurs with low-level digital audio. Noise-shaped dithering can provide the beneficial effects of dithering, but not be as noticeable—assuming listeners notice dithering at all (it's a subtle difference).

♦ Apply dithering only once: when converting a file to one with lower bit resolution.

♦ Applying data compression, which is more accurately called data omission, can reduce audio file size. The tradeoff is lower fidelity for smaller file sizes.

♦ The MP3 format is the most popular data compression format, although Apple's AAC is also popular because it's the default data compression for iTunes and the iPod.

♦ The FLAC format doesn't omit data, but doesn't reduce file size as much as lossy data compression algorithms.

Appendix A

Obtaining the Benefits of Higher Sample Rates in Lower-Sample-Rate Projects

The controversy about whether people can tell the difference between audio originally recorded at 96 kHz that's *played back* at 44.1 kHz or 96 kHz has never really been resolved. However, the sample rate *can* make a difference when recording sounds generated "in the box," for instance, using a virtual instrument plug-in that synthesizes a sound, or a distortion effect created by an amp simulator. In these cases, any improvement heard with high sample rates comes primarily from eliminating *foldover distortion*, also known as *aliasing*.

Although you can simply record at a high sample rate, as mentioned previously in the book, this isn't always desirable. Fortunately, there are two ways to obtain the benefits of high-sample-rate recording in low-sample-rate projects.

Solution 1

If a project contains only virtual instruments and no audio, you can temporarily change the sample rate within the recording software from 44.1 or 48 kHz to a higher rate, like 96 kHz. If the audio interface can adjust itself to the new sample rate, render (bounce or export) the audio tracks that benefit from the higher sample rate. This converts them into audio at the higher sample rate, so there won't be any foldover distortion. After rendering any sounds that benefit from the higher sample rate, change the sample rate back down to your original project rate of 44.1 or 48 kHz.

You don't lose the benefits of oversampling when you later convert the sample rate back down to 44.1 kHz, because rendering at the higher sample rate eliminates any foldover distortion in the audio range—and 44.1 kHz has no problem playing back sounds in the audio range. However, note that oversampling can't fix audio that already incorporates aliasing distortion.

Solution 2

You will not be able to change the song's sample rate easily if audio has already been recorded, so here's a foolproof method if Solution 1 doesn't work. Let's assume that we're using a 44.1 kHz project sampling rate; let's also assume that the virtual instrument's MIDI track has been finalized, but we haven't yet rendered it to audio.

Here's how to "oversample" virtual instruments:

1.   Save the virtual instrument settings as a preset so you can call it up in step 5.

2.   Export the MIDI clip driving the instrument. For best results, extend its beginning to the project beginning.

3.   Close the existing project.

4.   Create a new project at a higher sample rate, like 88.2 or 96 kHz.

5.   Insert the virtual instrument you used previously, and then load the preset you saved.

6.   Import the MIDI clip and assign it to the instrument track.

7.   Render the instrument track, starting at the song's beginning.

8.   Export the rendered audio; then close the project.

9.   Open the original project that uses a 44.1 kHz sample rate.

10.   Import the rendered audio; your recording software will convert the sample rate back down to 44.1 kHz during the import.

11.   Use this as the instrument audio instead of what would have resulted from rendering the instrument in the 44.1 kHz project.

Appendix B

Clocking and Networked Audio

As covered in Chapter 4, digital systems are based on particular sample rates. A *master clock* (also called *system clock*) determines the sample rate frequency, and for best results this clock needs to be as accurate and stable as possible. Furthermore, all digital audio devices should sync to this clock. For an analogy, consider the system clock as the drummer: all the other "musicians" (digital devices) get their timing cues from the beat established by this drummer. For the best rhythm, you want the drummer to be "in the pocket," and you want the other musicians to be able to follow the drummer's timing.

Your host software's preferences will allow you to specify a clock source. In most cases, clocking is handled transparently and you needn't think about it. The clock source will almost always default to internal, which means the software is receiving its clock signal from the audio interface (after all, the interface is already working at the desired sample rate).

Clocking With External Devices

If a second digital device feeds into an audio interface's digital input (e.g., S/PDIF or ADAT optical), then you will want to sync the interface to the second device's digital output. For example, if a unit with a S/PDIF digital output connects to an audio interface's S/PDIF digital input, the two devices need to synchronize, or there can be issues with the audio going out of sync (resulting in clicks or dropouts). Because the S/PDIF signal from the outboard unit is outputting a clock signal, you can have the audio interface sync to it by specifying S/PDIF as the clock source. If the interface were receiving a signal from an ADAT optical output instead, then you would specify ADAT optical as the clock source.

Here's an even more complex scenario. Suppose audio interface "A" has an ADAT digital input, and a second, ADAT-compatible audio interface "B" provides an additional eight mic preamps—you can connect its ADAT digital output to the digital input for interface "A." Now assume that you need *another* eight mic preamps, so you patch an expansion mic preamp unit "C" with eight preamps and an ADAT-compatible output into the interface "B" ADAT input. In the control panel for each device, you would set audio interface "A" to sync to the ADAT clock out from interface "B," and interface "B" to the ADAT output from expansion unit "C." Expansion unit "C" would provide the master clock for the system.

Word Clock

If you to need synchronize multiple pieces of gear where you can't just feed the clock out from one device into the clock input of another device (particularly in a system that includes video), *word clock* becomes relevant. This is an advanced topic, and you'll likely not need word clock in a home studio context. But it is part of the digital audio world, so let's take a look.

Note that word clock is *not* about improving audio quality; that may have been the case in the early days of digital audio, but it is no longer true. What word clock can do is make a complex system more stable and convenient to operate.

Where word clock really matters is audio systems that work with video, or in video post-production. This is because the audio sample rate must synchronize with the picture frame rate, so you need a master clock that transmits a reference sync signal for video, or syncs to a video reference and from there, drives the audio part of the system.

In higher-end digital audio systems, you'll typically find a stable master clock that outputs its clock signal over a *BNC connector* (the name comes from Bayonet Neill-Concelman, after its shape and designers). This clock signal typically gets "daisy-chained"—in other words, the master clock out feeds device A's clock input, device A's clock output feeds device B's clock input, device B's clock output feeds device C's clock input, and so on (Fig. B.1). This keeps the audio and video that is emanating from (or being received by) the various units in sync.

Figure B.1   The BNC In connector receives word clock, while the Out connector passes the word clock signal along to the next word clock input.

The last input in a word clock chain is *terminated*, meaning that it includes circuitry that tells the clock signal "this is the end of the line." (For the technically-minded, termination prevents the clock signal from reflecting back into the line.) Most digital audio devices intended for use with external clocks will have a termination switch at the input in case it's the last unit in the timing chain. (Incidentally, unlike AES/EBU,

S/PDIF, and ADAT, the MADI interface mentioned in Chapter 2 does not include a clock signal. It's necessary to use an external clock generator with MADI.)

In some digital audio systems, instead of using daisy-chaining, the clock goes through a distribution amplifier that feeds each input individually.

Fun stuff, eh?

Hey! Wake up!!

Networked Audio

There are two common ways to network audio, Dante (Digital Audio Network Through Ethernet) and AVB (Audio Video Bridging). These are intended primarily for commercial and professional applications, where many audio channels need to be sent to several locations, and/or sent over long distances. As such, it's not really that relevant to home studios unless you have, for example, a setup where you track at one end of a house and mix in a converted upstairs bedroom. Even then, more conventional approaches will often do what you need.

Getting deep into networked audio is beyond the scope of this book. However, there's an excellent article by Mitch Gallagher titled "Audio Networking Explained" at https://www.sweetwater.com/insync/audio-networking-explained/.

About the Author

Musician/author Craig Anderton is an internationally recognized authority on music and technology. His onstage career spans from the 60s with the group Mandrake, through the early 2000s with electronic groups Air Liquide and Rei$$dorf Force, to the "power duo" EV2 with Public Enemy's Brian Hardgroove, and EDM-oriented solo performances.

He has played on, produced, or mastered over 20 major label recordings, did pop music session work in New York in the 1970s on guitar and keyboards, played Carnegie Hall, and more recently, has mastered well over a hundred tracks for various artists.

In the mid-80s, Craig co-founded *Electronic Musician* magazine. As an author, he's written over 35 books on musical electronics and over a thousand articles for magazines like *Keyboard, Sound on Sound, Rolling Stone, Pro Sound News, Guitar Player, Mix,* and several European publications.

Craig has lectured on technology and the arts (in 10 countries, 38 U.S. states, and three languages), and done sound design work for companies like Alesis, Gibson, Peavey, PreSonus, Roland, and Steinberg.

Please check out some of his music at youtube.com/thecraiganderton, visit his web site at craiganderton.com, and follow him on twitter @craig_anderton.